INCREASING ACADEMIC ACHIEVEMENT WITH THE TRIVIUM OF CLASSICAL EDUCATION

INCREASING ACADEMIC ACHIEVEMENT WITH THE TRIVIUM OF CLASSICAL EDUCATION

✦

Its Historical Development, Decline in the Last Century, and Resurgence in Recent Decades

Randall D. Hart, Ph.D.

iUniverse, Inc.
New York Lincoln Shanghai

INCREASING ACADEMIC ACHIEVEMENT WITH THE TRIVIUM OF CLASSICAL EDUCATION

Its Historical Development, Decline in the Last Century, and Resurgence in Recent Decades

iUniverse books may be ordered through booksellers or by contacting:

iUniverse
2021 Pine Lake Road, Suite 100
Lincoln, NE 68512
www.iuniverse.com
1-800-Authors (1-800-288-4677)

ISBN-13: 978-0-595-38169-2 (pbk)
ISBN-13: 978-0-595-82536-3 (ebk)
ISBN-10: 0-595-38169-3 (pbk)
ISBN-10: 0-595-82536-2 (ebk)

Printed in the United States of America

This book is dedicated to:

Jan, my wonderful wife of 32 years;

Our children and their spouses:

Ashley, Jamie and Heather Hart, Andrea and Chris Hill;

And our grandchild:

Sydnie

Contents

CHAPTER 1   Introduction 1

CHAPTER 2   Philosophical and Curricular Foundations of Education 3

     Philosophy of Idealism 5

     Philosophy of Realism. 6

     Philosophy of Pragmatism. 8

CHAPTER 3   The Historical Development of the Trivium 10

     The Life of Socrates. 10
     469–399 B.C.

     The Life of Plato 12
     427–347 B.C.

     Life of Aristotle 17
     384–322 B.C.

     Life of Isocrates 21
     436–338 B.C.

     The Life of Quintilian. 24
     35–95 A.D.

     The Life of Saint Augustine. 31
     354–430 A.D.

     Life of Cassiodorus 38
     485–585 A.D.

CHAPTER 4   The Rise of Universities. 41

     Origins of the Medieval University 42

     The Early Universities. 43

     Curriculum 47

Significance of the Medieval University 52

Famous Scholastic Instructors 53

Peter Abelard 53

Thomas Aquinas 55

CHAPTER 5   Decline of Classical Education **57**

The Enlightenment 58

Francis Bacon 58

John Locke 60

Jean-Jacques Rousseau 61

Emmanuel Kant 62

Johann Pestalozzi 62

Frederick Froebel 62

William James and Pragmatism 63

John Dewey and Educational Progressivism 67

CHAPTER 6   The Resurgence of Classical Education **71**

• *Life of Dorothy L. Sayers and "The Lost Tools of Learning"* *71*

"The Lost Tools" of Learning: What Are They and Why Are They So
     Important? 76

Grammar Stage 77

Logic, or Dialectic Stage 79

Rhetoric Stage 80

Doug Wilson and *Recovering the Lost Tools of Learning* 81

• *Mortimer Adler and The Paideia Proposal* *82*

Adler's Background 82

The Paideia Proposal 84

Purpose of School 85

Curriculum 86

Column One: Acquisition of Knowledge 86

Column Two: Development of Skills 87

Column Three: Enlargement of the Understanding 88

The Role of the Teacher 89

Role of the Student 89

CHAPTER 7   Implementation of the Model and Concluding
Remarks 91

The Challenge of Teaching in a Classical School. 91

The Sieve of Classical Philosophy 92

Table 1: Cassiodorus' Topics of Study from: An Introduction to Divine and
Human Readings. 97

Table 2. Student-Centered Instruction versus Teacher-Centered Instruction 99

Table 3: The Three Columns 101

APPENDIX   The Lost Tools of Learning. 103

Recommended Readings 121

References. 127

Index. 133

Acknowledgements

First of all I wish to thank Jim and Dayle Seneff for providing the academic fellowship that enabled me to complete my Ph.D. and write this book. Without their financial support, none of this would have been possible. I also wish to thank Dr. Luder Whitlock for his support, supervision, and encouragement during this endeavor. Dr. Whitlock, the former president of Reformed Theological Seminary, is truly a man to be emulated—being filled with kindness, compassion, and a true servant's heart.

Special thanks also to my wonderful son, Jamie, who shared his office space with me during the writing of this book and patiently answered all my questions about how to use my new Apple laptop.

1

Introduction

I had the occasion to read Doug Wilson's book entitled *Recovering the Lost Tools of Learning: An Approach to Distinctively Christian Education* in 1992, while flying to Chicago. I was somewhat familiar with classical education based on the writings of an educational hero of mine, Mortimer Adler, a well-known philosopher. In the '80s, Adler had developed a classical approach to education that could be used in any given public school in America. However, I must admit that Wilson's title piqued my interest. What were the tools of learning to which he referred? If they had been lost, why should they be recovered? These and other questions raced through my mind as I delved into a book that would profoundly shape my beliefs regarding education.

This book provides students, teachers, and parents with a brief summation of classical education and its history. Much of what has been written about classical education in the past several years is specifically targeted for Christian schools and home schooling parents. One reason for writing this book is to share the dream that classical education is a model that can be effectively used by all educators, not just those in private Christian education.

Two models of classical education that have had a significant effect on the reemergence of classical schools across this country—classical education as advocated by Mortimer Adler in his book *The Paideia Proposal* and the use of the trivium as espoused by Dorothy L. Sayers in her essay "The Lost Tools of Learning"—will be reviewed.

Adler was a prolific writer, philosopher, and advocate of the "Great Book" approach, while Sayers is well known as a mystery writer and a translator of Dante's *Divine Comedy*. However, in order to understand Adler's and Sayers' approaches to classical education, one must have a basic understanding of the philosophical ideologies that have driven their work. In addition to the classical philosophies of idealism and realism, the more recent philosophy of pragmatism must also be reviewed as it was the direct catalyst for John Dewey's approach to education that so directly impacted the decline of classical education during the past century.

Chapter 3 provides a brief summation of key philosophers and teachers who greatly impacted the development of classical education from the Hellenistic Age to the Middle Ages. In her famous essay Sayers did a magnificent job of describing the trivium that was so masterfully employed during the Middle Ages, but she failed to provide for us insight into the historical development of these great tools of learning. One must only assume that when she was making her now famous address at Oxford she was addressing an audience that she believed understood the necessary philosophical prerequisites for understanding her speech. Although most Classical and Christian schools in the United States embrace Sayers' approach to education, it is highly unlikely that most teachers and parents have an adequate understanding of the history of the trivium.

In a brief format this book will seek to answer the following questions:

1. What is a classical, or liberal arts education, and what are the philosophies that under gird it?

2. What is "progressive" education and how has the movement impacted classical education during the past 100 years?

3. What are the tools of the trivium and how, when, and where did they originate?

4. What is the purpose of a classical education?

5. What type of curriculum should be used in classical schools?

6. What is the role of the teacher in a classical school?

7. What is the role of the student in classical education?

It is my hope and prayer that all who embrace classical education will continue to prove Miss Sayers wrong regarding one of her opening statements in her famous essay in which she stated, "However, it is in the highest degree improbable that the reforms I propose will ever be carried into effect."

2

Philosophical and Curricular Foundations of Education

I know you will be tempted to skip this section. Unfortunately, it is the rare person among us who truly enjoys reading philosophy. This is one of the sad results of the near demise of classical education in our country. However, students in our classical schools would probably tell you the study of philosophy is actually invigorating and deeply satisfying in their quest to answer the meaningful questions of life. Please hang in there, as it is very brief!

When I began teaching 27 years ago, my "philosophy of education" was quite simplistic—philosophy was for those professors in academia who spent their time discussing the questions of life that certainly had nothing to do with teaching in an elementary school. Early in my teaching career, was I a traditional teacher or a progressivist? At the time, I was not only unable to answer the question, but I was also simply not interested in doing so. The greatest aspect of being a teacher was to provide me with the opportunity to coach basketball.

When I reflect on my undergraduate education, the only educational methodology I was exposed to was the "open-classroom" approach. I knew this approach was child-centered versus teacher-centered, but I did not fully understand the implications of this terminology. Upon securing a 5th grade teaching position, my instincts told me to be wary of using such methodology in the strict parochial environment in which I found myself. Knowing that my performance would be to a great extent evaluated on classroom management, I certainly did not dare to allow my students the freedom to focus their studies on topics of their interests.

In 1987, I read E.D. Hirsch's book entitled, *Cultural Literacy*, which would have a profound effect on the importance I placed on embracing a philosophy of education. Hirsch placed a tremendous amount of importance on the "content" of education. As Americans we share a common culture, and thus we must share a common knowledge level in order to relate effectively with one another. Hirsch acknowledged that determining what each American should know is difficult to ascertain, but is certainly not to be left to America's youth to determine.

Around this same time, Allan Bloom's educational classic, *The Closing of the American Mind* (1987), catapulted to the forefront. Professor Bloom lamented the continued decline of the importance placed on receiving a "liberal arts" education. While Hirsch noted that most Americans could not identify the time frame of the Civil War, let alone its causes, Bloom sadly acknowledged that the so-called "learned" Americans of today could no longer make substantial analogies to such entities as Shakespearean plays or participate in the "great conversation" of our Western heritage.

In 1982, Mortimer Adler, one of America's most well-known philosophers, along with several prominent educators, produced a short book entitled *The Paideia Proposal*. Dr. Adler was highly critical of our educational system's emphasis on sharing information with our students, while failing to adequately teach the necessary skills of reading and writing. While teachers claim to emphasize higher level thinking skills, proper "coaching" and Socratic techniques are blatantly missing in our K-12 schools.

These particular books served as a catalyst in convincing me that all teachers must embrace a philosophy of education in order to become effective teachers. Every educational decision made and all consequential actions must be the result of intensive scrutiny. While operating under the premise that we as teachers must always do what is best for our students, we must always focus on "why" an action has or should be taken.

What follows in this section are brief summations of three major philosophies that have influenced theories of education. However, first we must have basic operating definitions for several key concepts of philosophy.

Basic Terminology

The following definitions were taken from *Routledge Encyclopedia of Philosophy* (2000). The philosophy of education employs the basic terms metaphysics, epistemology, and axiology.

Metaphysics examines the nature of ultimate reality. There is no single agreed-upon definition of reality. For example, is there life after death? Educators define reality according to their educational and theological philosophies.

Epistemology, which deals with knowledge and knowing, is closely related to methods of teaching and learning. Again, different philosophies hold different epistemological conceptions. Idealists see knowing, or cognition, as the recall of ideas that are latent in the mind. For them, the Socratic dialogue is the most appropriate teaching method.

Axiology seeks to prescribe what is of value. Axiology is divided into ethics and aesthetics. Ethics examines moral values and the rules of right conduct; aesthetics addresses values in beauty and art. Idealists and realists subscribe to the objective theory of value, which asserts that the good, true, and beautiful are universally valid in all places and at all times.

Philosophy of Idealism

Historical Development

Idealism is one of the oldest schools of philosophic thought. Plato, who is generally regarded as the father of idealism in the West, lived approximately 2,500 years ago; since then, the philosophy has been propounded, in various forms, by many others. In recent times, idealism has greatly impacted the writings of Mortimer Adler (1982), Robert Hutchins (1936), former president of the University of Chicago, and Allan Bloom, professor and author of *The Closing of the American Mind* (1987).

Metaphysics

Idealism emphasizes moral and spiritual reality as the primary sources of explanation of the universe. Truth and values are seen as absolute and universal. Knowledge is in the mind, and needs only to be brought to the conscious level through introspection. To know is to rethink the latent ideas that are already present in the mind. Such ideas are *a priori*; that is, they exist in our minds and through introspection the individual retrieves them. Aristotle believed these latent ideas were the result of a higher will, or universal mind, that he referred to as the "Unmoved Mover." St. Augustine believed that the possession of innate, or *a priori*, ideas somewhat defines what it means that we were created in God's image with the capability of attaining knowledge of his creation.

The idealist curriculum, constituting the cultural heritage of humankind, is hierarchical. At the top are the most general disciplines, philosophy and theology. Mathematics is especially valuable because it cultivates the power to deal with abstractions. History and literature also rank high because they are sources of moral and cultural models, exemplars, and heroes. Somewhat lower in curricular priority are the natural and physical sciences, which address particular cause-and-effect relationships. Since it is necessary for communication, language is an essential tool at all levels of learning.

Epistemology

The idealist would say that thinking and learning are names for the process of bringing ideas to consciousness. An appropriate means for doing this is the Socratic Method, a process by which the teacher stimulates the learner's awareness of ideas by asking leading questions.

History would be viewed as a means of studying the contributions made by great women and men of the past. Teachers would expose students to the classics—great and enduring works of art, literature, and music—so they can experience and share in the values conveyed by these cultural works from generation to generation.

Axiology

To the idealist, values reflect the good inherent in the universe. They are absolute, eternal, and universal. The role of the teacher is to help students explore the basic ideas that provide answers to the questions Socrates and Plato first asked: What is truth? What is beauty? What is the good life? These answers, although hidden, are present in our minds, and we need to reflect deeply to bring them forth. Thus education is about ideas and is an intellectual undertaking. This perspective rejects the consumerism, vocationalism, and the god of relativism that pervades our contemporary society.

Philosophy of Realism

Historical Development

Realism is another of the classical schools of thought. Aristotle was a major contributor to the development of this philosophy in ancient Greece. The realist sees the world primarily in material terms. This world of things exists independently of the mind. Revelation is experienced through sensory experience and the use of reason.

Metaphysics

The realist views reality in terms of the world of nature. Everything is derived from nature and is subject to its laws. Realism suggests that life in its physical, mental, moral, and spiritual sense is attributable to and explicable by the ordinary operations of the natural world. Realism is more concerned with things as they are than with things as they should be.

Epistemology

The classical realist sees reality as universal, abstract, and permanent. Reality is discovered by seeking to understand the essence, or nature of visible objects. Less emphasis is placed on the Platonic world of ideas.

Like the idealist, the realist believes that a curriculum consisting of organized, separate subject matter is the most effective and efficient way of learning about reality. History, language, science, and mathematics are the primary organized bodies of knowledge.

The school is the institution that has been established to teach students about the objective world. Realists develop educational aims that define the school's role as primarily academic. Students should learn subjects that will help them understand their world so that they can live full and satisfying lives.

Realist educators welcome standards that require students and teachers to demonstrate mastery of academic subject matter. They would argue that genuine quality of education requires teachers who are competent in the subjects that they teach and have a broad background in the liberal arts and sciences. This l enables the teacher to point out relationships between her or his own area of expertise and other subject matter areas. Because of this stress on teachers' knowledge, realists favor competency testing in teacher-education programs. Realist teachers also tend to believe in competency testing for students. Realists would also oppose those activities that interfere with the school's primary function as a center of academic learning.

Realist teachers employ a wide variety of teaching methods such as lecture, discussion, demonstration, or experiment. Mastery of content is extremely important, and methodology is a subordinate means of obtaining the primary goal.

Axiology

Ronald Nash, a philosopher and professor at Reformed Theological Seminary in Orlando, illuminated the meaning of realism by juxtaposing it with antirealism. He stated that he is a realist in respect to universals, properties, states of affairs, numbers, mind, truth, and God. However, he is an antirealist in regards to mermaids, unicorns, golden mountains, square circles, and Tinker Bell. The level of humor regarding a joke or the concept of "beauty is in the eye of the beholder" is more difficult to classify. One's understanding of moral values is certainly dictated by philosophical beliefs. The realist would embrace objective moral standards while the antirealist would have his or her foundation in relativism. (1999, p. 236)

Philosophy of Pragmatism

For supporters of classical education, it is extremely important to possess an understanding of pragmatism, as I would contend that it was one of the major contributors to the near collapse of classical education for the past 120 years. Proponents of Classical and Christian education benefit by embracing aspects of idealism and realism. However, embracing the philosophy of pragmatism and its resulting educational belief system known as progressivism would represent the antithesis of a classical education. Thus the age old maxim of "knowing thine enemy" certainly is applicable.

Historical Development

Pragmatism is a distinctly American contribution to the general field of philosophy. With the advent of the industrial revolution and experimental science, as a nation we became less respectful of tradition or any religion that would support the status quo. Temporal existence as a value in itself became more prominent. Charles Sander Peirce (1839-1914) who was once a student at Harvard and became a lecturer at John Hopkins University was the first to use the term "pragmatism." The term originated from *pragma*, the Greek word for action or deed. Peirce believed that if an idea could not be utilized in a practical situation, then it had no meaning (Titus, 1953).

William James (1842-1910) also played a significant role in the development of pragmatism. He believed that pragmatism could be a methodology for settling philosophical disputes. Whatever ideas worked or had "cash value" were necessarily true. He was opposed to *a priori* beliefs and to the Calvinistic belief of a sovereign God (Howick, 1971).

John Dewey (1859-1952) is credited with applying the principles of pragmatism to all aspects of life, thus developing it into a complete system of thought. He believed that moral authority could not be based on a fixed goal since no two ethical situations were the same. Also, historically fixed subject matter was detrimental to society because it only served to maintain the status quo. (Howick, 1971).

Metaphysics

Pragmatism does not concern itself with reason or mental realities. Experience is used to relate men to ideas of the here and now. Because the historical past is not deemed to be important, strong emphasis is placed on continually seeking change. Pragmatism has a close relationship to the ancient philosophy of the Greek, Heraclitus who lived in the 5th century B.C. He believed that "everything is in flux" like the flowing of water in a river.

Epistemology

Because there is no innate truth, man does not discover knowledge, he creates it. Something can be true only if proven to be workable. An idea that does not yield satisfactory results thus is false. One establishes truth by seeking desirable consequences.

Axiology

Values are relative and primarily temporal. Ethics and aesthetics are specific to the individual and thus relative. However, preservation of democracy rates very high, especially with Dewey, because it allows for the lifestyle that fosters human freedom, character, and intelligence. Dewey's educational beliefs, known as "progressivism," are explored in greater detail in chapter 5, which deals with the near demise of classical education.

3

The Historical Development of the Trivium

We now begin our exploration of philosophers and educators from the past who have greatly impacted the development of classical education. The list is not exhaustive, and certainly those more learned than I may not accept my arbitrary list. For my study, I selected famous philosophers who helped develop and carry on the tradition of a classical education through their own teachings and establishment of schools. For example, some might add Cicero to this list since he indeed was one of the most famous rhetoricians of all time. However, his primary purpose was not in functioning as a teacher and promoter of schools.

The Life of Socrates

Socrates was born in Athens circa 469 B.C. He is remembered as the most influential sophist of his time, although he lived in poverty and publicly disdained material possessions. He successfully served as a hoplite in the army and did manage to support a wife and several children. While he may have inherited some money, he also received gifts from wealthy supporters. He paid little attention to his physical appearance and was considered to be quite homely. He sported the same cloak during the summer and winter.

Two important facts about Socrates are that he lived for philosophy and was killed on anti-intellectual grounds. He was charged with introducing new gods and corrupting the youth. Impiety ranked as an extremely serious crime because the gods were believed to punish the entire city for the actions of even on person.

As usual in Athenian trials, no judge presided to rule on what evidence was admissible or how the law should be applied. The accusers argued their case against Socrates before a jury of 501 men that had been assembled.

The prosecution of Socrates had both a religious and a moral component. Religiously, the prosecutors accused Socrates of not believing in the gods of the city-state and of introducing new divinities. Morally, they charged, he had led the young men of Athens away from Athenian conventions and ideals. After the conclusion of the prosecutors' remarks, Socrates spoke in his own defense, as required by Athenian legal procedure. In the *Apology*, Plato presented Socrates as taking this occasion not to rebut all the charges or try to curry favor or beg for sympathy, as jurors expected in serious cases, but to reiterate his unyielding dedication to goading his fellow citizens into examining their preconceptions. This irritating process of constant questioning, he maintained, would help them learn to live virtuous lives. Furthermore, they should care not about their material possessions but about making their true selves, their souls, as good as possible. If he were to be acquitted, he baldly stated, he vowed to remain their stinging gadfly no matter what the consequences to himself.

After Socrates was convicted, the prosecutors proposed death, but Socrates was entitled to propose exile as an alternative, which the jury probably would have accepted. Socrates, however, responded by claiming that he should be rewarded rather than punished. The jury chose death (Plato, *Apology*).

Socrates' Impact on Classical Education

The sophists were a poorly defined group of itinerant teachers who disagreed on philosophical and pedagogical specifics and never established schools in the traditional sense. Their services were sought by the new monied class who tried to use the power of rhetoric in their quest to solidify their economic position. The sophists sought to develop persuasive techniques as opposed to wrestling with serious philosophical issues. They specialized in educational areas that would later become known as the trivium of the Roman and medieval ages. For the sophists, grammar was studied in order to understand and express ideas clearly, logic served to help in clarifying one's thoughts, while rhetoric allowed one to be persuasive through the power of speech (Gutek, 1972).

Socrates' passion was to discover guidelines for leading a just life and was the first philosopher to make ethics and morality his central concern. If Socrates did record any of his ideas, none of his writings has survived. What we do know of him comes from others' writings, especially those of his pupil Plato. Plato is famous for his "dialogues" that present Socrates and others in extended conversation about philosophy. Plato presented Socrates as a relentless questioner of his fellow citizens, foreign friends, and various sophists.

Socrates' questions were intended to make his interlocutors examine the basic assumptions of their way of life. Employing what has become known over time as the Socratic Method, Socrates did not just provide direct instruction; instead, he led his students to draw conclusions in response to his probing questions, while he refuted their assumptions.

Socrates typically began one of his conversations by asking the interlocutor to define a concept such as happiness or courage. For instance, in Plato's dialogue entitled Laches, after the Athenian general who appears as one of the dialogue's participants, Socrates asked the interlocutors what constitutes a brave soldier. Socrates then proceeded by further questioning to show that the definitions stated by the interlocutors actually conflict with their other beliefs concerning what defines true courage. This indirect method of searching for the truth often left Socrates' conversational partners bewildered because they realized they were ignorant regarding an idea they thought they knew perfectly well. Socrates believed that he indeed was the wisest of all men because he openly acknowledged that he did not know everything.

He stated that education should make a man happier and able to become a better citizen. He taught that the most valuable thing a man could have was knowledge. He asserted that true knowledge of justice would lead people to choose good over evil and thus become equipped to live happy lives.

Socrates passionately believed that just behavior was better for human beings than injustice and that morality was justified because it created happiness and well-being. Essentially, he argued that just behavior, or virtue, was identical to knowledge and that true knowledge of justice would inevitably lead people to choose good over evil and therefore to have truly happy lives.

The Life of Plato

Plato was born in 427 or 428 B.C. and died at the age of eighty. Plato's real name may have been Aristocles, with "Plato" being a nickname that may have meant "the broader," derived either from the width of his shoulders, the results of training for wrestling, or from the size of his forehead.

Following the loss to Sparta in the Peloponnesian War, the former democratic government was replaced by an oligarchy. Plato had the opportunity to join those in power, but he refused. These men, who later became known as the Thirty Tyrants, soon proved to be ruthless rulers. This may well have served as a catalyst for Plato's desire to develop an educational system that produced wise and moral leaders.

Plato was a dedicated and passionate student of Socrates during his twenties as this well-known quote exhibits: "I thank God that I was born Greek and not barbarian, freeman and not slave, man and not woman; but above all, that I was born in the age of Socrates" (cited in Durant, 1953, p. 13).

The execution of Socrates in 399 B.C. had a profound effect on him; he decided that he would have nothing further to do with politics in Athens. His friends implored him to leave Athens for his own safety and to explore the world. Scholars debate exactly where his travels took him. He may have first traveled to Egypt, followed by Sicily, and then on to Italy where he studied at the school founded many years before by the famous Pythagoras. Here he came to appreciate the value of mathematics.

On his return to Athens in 387 BC, Plato founded his famous university called the "Academy" on land containing a grove of olive trees that had been dedicated to the Greek hero, Academos. Plato presided over his Academy in Athens, an institution devoted to research and instruction in philosophy and the sciences, until his death in 348 B.C. (Marrou, 1956).

His reasons for setting up the Academy were connected with his earlier ventures into politics. He had been bitterly disappointed with the standards displayed by those in public office and he hoped to train, in his Academy, young men who would become statesmen. Plato thought that these men would be able to improve the political leadership of the cities of Greece. Plato's Academy flourished until 529 AD when the Christian emperor Justinian closed it down because it was a pagan establishment. Having survived for 900 years, it is the longest surviving school known.

Plato's Impact on Classical Education

Plato's theory of knowledge, or epistemology, was based on the doctrine of "reminiscence," by which man recalls truths, or ideas, that are within the minds of all men. The shock of merging one's soul with a temporal body causes man to forget the knowledge of truth. Nevertheless, this latent knowledge of ideal forms of justice and goodness can be resurrected and brought to consciousness through a proper education.

Plato was an idealist because of the tremendous importance he placed on the concept of *ideas*. For Plato the primary reality was the world of ideas. This metaphysical realm was even more important to Plato than the world of physical objects. For Plato, true knowledge existed in the realm of ideas. For example, as I write these words, my laptop is placed on a table. According to Plato, there exists in the metaphysical world the perfect concept of "table." Any attempt to reproduce a table in the physical realm is simply a mere shadow of the essence of the idea of table.

In his theory of *forms*, Plato rejected the changeable, deceptive world that we are aware of through our senses (a posteriori). Instead, he asserted that knowledge is ascertained through reason (a priori). R.C. Sproul, in his book entitled *Consequences of Ideas*, summarized Plato's concept of knowledge this way:

> For Plato, knowledge comes, not from experience (a posteriori) but through reason (a priori). Ultimate ideas are innate and not discovered from experience. The best the senses can do is to awaken the consciousness to what it already knows. At worst the senses can mislead the mind. Teaching is a form of midwifery, in which the teacher only assists the student in giving birth to an idea that is already there. (Sproul, 2000, pp. 37-38)

Plato also believed that concepts such as beauty or justice exist in the *ideal* world. However, artistic productions that we consider to be beautiful fall far short of imitating reality. The greatest artist painting the most beautiful picture cannot duplicate true beauty. He can only produce a rendering that correlates with the level of recall regarding the innate concept within his mind.

Understanding Plato's philosophical views is difficult because he did not write a systematic treatise giving his views; rather he wrote about 30 dialogues. Within the dialogues, Plato does not appear as a character. Therefore, we cannot ascertain if Plato's assertions truly represent his own views. Socrates usually appeared as the protagonist, so it is not clear how much these characters expressed views with which they themselves would have put forward. It is commonly held that the thoughts expressed by Socrates in the early dialogues represented views actually held by Socrates.

Plato's contributions to the theories of education are exemplified by the way that he conducted the Academy and through his ideas of what constituted an educated person. He also contributed to logic and legal philosophy, including rhetoric. Although Plato made no important mathematical discoveries himself, his belief that mathematics provided the finest training for the mind was extremely important in the development of the subject. Over the door of the Academy was written: *"Let no one unversed in geometry enter here."*

Plato's Proposed Plan of Instruction

Unlike the Sophists, who saw the role of education as producing immediate practical results, Plato believed that the fundamental purpose of education was the conquest of truth by rational knowledge. From a political perspective, Plato purposed to train an ideal "king" who would be distinguished by his rational knowledge of science and government, attained through genuine knowledge based on reasoning (Marrou, 1956).

According to Plato, education was not simply imparting information or developing skills. The teacher was to help turn the eyes of the student's soul to genuine reality in the quest for truth while stimulating his love of the good, the true, and the beautiful through the development of correct habits (Gutek, 1972). In Plato's ideal world, children were to be separated from their parents and placed in state nurseries until the age of six. Plato believed that parents were too often a corrupting influence on the lives of their children. Prejudice and ignorance would necessarily be passed on to the children by too much time being spent with parents. (A case could certainly be made that this disrespect for parenthood exists among some governmental agencies today as well.) During this time, boys and girls were to play supervised educational games in a type of kindergarten environment (Plato, *Leges I*, 643 bc).

Formal education was to begin at the age of seven with students studying music, mathematics, and gymnastics until the age of eighteen.

Music

The study of music in Plato's day was broadly conceived as compared to today's understanding. Music then included reading, writing, choral singing, and dancing (Plato, *Leges VII*, 809 b). Plato believed that music was worthwhile for intrinsic enjoyment, but it was also worthwhile in helping to provide an attractive form for learning the content of math, history, and science (Durant, 1953). Thus, even today, musical chants and jingles are widely used in an effective manner within classical schools. After mastering the basic literary skills of reading and writing, students would read carefully selected classics, but Plato strongly opposed using the works of Homer. Because literature was to be used in the formation of character, Plato condemned the writers of mythology for how they portrayed the gods and heroes.

Plato believed that music lent grace and health to the soul and body, but too much music was dangerous. To be merely a musician, without developing athletic skills, caused one to be "melted and softened beyond what was good" (Plato, *Republic*, 410).

Mathematics

Plato believed that mathematics should be taught at every stage, even the most elementary. Initially students were to be taught counting skills and then move on to solving problems based on real-life situations. Students would also be introduced to the basic aspects of geometry, such as determining area and volume, along with a basic understanding of astronomy and the development of calendars (Plato, *Laws VII*, 809 bc).

Plato agreed with Hippias that no other subject could compare with mathematics because it awakened the mind and developed liveliness and memorization powers (Diogenes Laertius, VIII, 87). Unlike many of his successors and some modern-day educators, Plato believed that everyone could learn basic mathematics, at least at the grammar stage.

Although, he did contend that only the truly gifted were able to complete the arduous task of mastering higher-level mathematics (Plato, *Laws VII*, 818 a).

Plato believed that mathematics provided the best litmus test for the people who would one day be ready to study philosophy (Plato, *Republic*, 526 c). Tests such as the SAT and ACT would certainly indicate such a modern-day competitive system is still in place. Plato would apparently agree with using one's mastery of mathematics as a major criterion for college placement.

Gymnastics

Although gymnastics continued from infancy to adulthood, Plato advocated interrupting strictly intellectual studies at the age of eighteen. For the next two years, students would be involved in "compulsory gymnastic service", or as we might say "they were drafted into the military."

Following military service, only a select number of students would continue with formal education. Durant stated that if such a system were in place today, Plato would have those who failed to make this "select" team become our business personnel, clerks, factory workers, and farmers. This prestigious group would receive ten more years of education and training, with a strong emphasis on moral development. Following a demanding test, those who failed would become the business executives and military leaders (Durant, 1953).

From the age of thirty to thirty-five, the remaining students were to study the discipline of dialectic. Finally, at the age of 35 they would be allowed the great privilege of studying philosophy for the next fifteen years. At this point, they would be deemed ready and capable of becoming the elite rulers of the country whom Plato called philosopher-kings. Thus, according to Plato, one cannot become truly wise until attaining the age of fifty.

Life of Aristotle

Aristotle was born in 384 B.C. in the small Greek town of Stagira in Macedonia, and so he later came to be known as "the Stagirite." He was the son of Nicomachus, who was the court physician of King Amyntas II (grandfather of Alexander the Great). Aristotle had a life-long passion for science that he may have inherited from his father. It is possible that Aristotle received training in dissection and may have helped his father in surgery.

With Plato at the Academy

Undoubtedly, he demonstrated precociousness for learning, because at the age of seventeen he was sent to complete his education in Athens. In 367, Aristotle began his studies at Plato's renowned school, The Academy. There Aristotle remained for the next twenty years.

It is clear that in Plato he found the philosopher who would so greatly influence his life. Aristotle did not implicitly accept all of Plato's philosophical beliefs. However, Plato and Aristotle had a great mutual respect for each other. At one time Plato is alleged to have called Aristotle "the reader par excellence and the mind of the school." Later their relations may have been less cordial, but during Plato's leadership of the Academy Aristotle remained loyal.

Departure from Athens and the Academy

After Plato's death in 347, Aristotle left the Academy. One may speculate that this decision was influenced by his disappointment in not being named as Plato's successor. Accompanied by Xenocrates, who would several years later become the head of the Academy, Aristotle accepted an invitation to visit a former fellow-student in the Academy. This friend, Hermeias, had risen from being a slave to become the ruler of Atarneus and Assos in Mysia. The next three years were spent with a small group of Platonic friends.

Next, Aristotle moved to Mytilene on the island of Lesbos. There Aristotle is reputed to have conducted much of his scientific research, especially in marine biology. While living in Mytilene, Aristotle supposedly received the invitation from Philip to come to Pella, the capital of Macedonia, to tutor Philip's son, now known as Alexander the Great, the future conqueror of the then known world. For the next six years, Aristotle remained in Pella as Alexander's private tutor.

Return to Athens and the Founding of the Lyceum School

By 336, Aristotle had left Pella and returned to Athens for what has sometimes been called the third major phase in his life. Being passed over again for the directorship of the Academy, Aristotle—perhaps with financing from Alexander himself—decided to found his own school, which came to be known as the Lyceum. Unlike Plato's Academy, which was primarily devoted to mathematics and political philosophy, the Lyceum had a tendency to emphasize biology and the natural sciences. Athenaeus informed us that Alexander the Great made contributions to the school of 800 talents to be used for facilities and research. In today's financial market, this amount would exceed many millions of dollars (in Durant, 1953). He chose as its home a group of gymnasiums dedicated to Apollo Lyceus, the god of shepherds. Here, every morning, he walked up and down the tree-covered paths with his pupils and discussed the questions of philosophy. Hence from these famous walks (peripator) developed the title, "the peripatetic school." As Sproul pointed out, this method of lecturing to disciples following close behind was used by others, with the most famous being Jesus of Nazareth (2000).

Aristotle presided over the Lyceum for thirteen years. While involved in scientific studies, his literary output was massive. He was the author of treatises on physics, astronomy, zoology, biology, botany, psychology, logic, ethics, politics, and metaphysics.

End of His Life in Exile

On the death of Alexander in 323, an outbreak of anti-Macedonian feeling ensued, and Aristotle's connections with Philip and Alexander incited antipathy toward him. It is also possible that the hostility of the Platonic and Isocratean schools conspired against him. Unfortunately, like Socrates, an absurd charge of impiety was brought against him. Reportedly stating that he would not let the Athenians "sin twice against philosophy," he withdrew to Chalcis where he died in 322.

Aristotle's Impact on Classical Education

The Preservation of Aristotle's Writings

Following his death, Aristotle has continued to impact education and philosophy in a cyclical manner for over two thousand years. The world is fortunate that the corpus of Aristotle's writings have even survived, although we cannot state that we today possess the properly published writings of Aristotle. What survives today are his notes that Aristotle himself prepared or his students jotted down during his lectures.

After Aristotle's death, his library, including his own treatises, passed into the hands of Theophrastus, Aristotle's successor as director of the Lyceum. Theophrastus then bequeathed the library to the son of one of Aristotle's friends in Assos, and he hid the manuscripts in an underground cellar or cave, fearing that the books might be seized for the royal library at Pergamum. So effectively were they hidden that the books themselves remained lost for over a hundred years. Eventually taken to Rome, they were catalogued and edited by Andronicus of Rhodes in the first century B.C. (Rubenstein, 2004).

Following the decline of Rome, Aristotle's writings were scattered and lost, and his philosophy fell into almost total eclipse in the Western world. Fortunately for mankind, his work had in the meanwhile spread to the Arab world, where his philosophy came to be both enthusiastically and perceptively pursued by many Arab thinkers and scholars. Because of the Crusades, Westerners were reunited with Aristotle, and his writings helped to usher in the "the great thaw" of the celebrated twelfth century revival of learning.

Aristotle on Form and Matter

Frequently cited as the founder of Western philosophical realism, Aristotle asserted that all objects are composed of form and matter and exist independently of man's knowledge of them. Aristotle did not endorse Plato's belief that the form of something exists in some sort of non-physical world. Plato would argue that a table can be constructed but its essence exists in the metaphysical concept of table. Aristotle would state that a table consists of matter and form in a complementary and necessary fashion (Gottlieb, 2000).

Man is endowed with form, defined as soul or mind, and with matter, the corporal body. Unlike his fellow animals, man possesses the power of rationality. For Aristotle, the good or virtuous man is one who activates this rational potentiality to its fullest extent. Reflectiveness and rationality guide his ethical behavior and decision-making (Gutek, 1972).

For man, the universal quest is happiness—the "summum bonum," or the "good at which all things aim." Thus, every moral action is designed to realize some good end or purpose (Gutek, 1972, p. 41).

He recommended three modes of life: the life of pleasure, the life of sociality, and the life of contemplation. As a result he developed his theory regarding moderation—his "Golden Mean."

The Unmoved Mover or God

Aristotle viewed the universe as eternal but everlastingly undergoing change. This lead him to question the cause of everlasting change. He attributed all changes occurring on earth to the motion of the heavenly bodies. But to what or to whom does he assign this ultimate power? What was the initial cause? Aristotle reasoned that the heavenly bodies could not be held in place by an entity that itself was in motion or ever changed in any way. If this were the case, this entity too would have needed a cause for its change or motion. Thus, Aristotle understood that the ultimate cause of motion must be an uncaused cause or an unmoved mover.

Sproul conveyed that this formed the classical basis for the idea that "God" is a logically necessary being. Later philosophical theology would add that God is necessary ontologically as well. God is self-existent and cannot *not* be. That is, pure being has its power of being within itself (Sproul, 2000).

Aristotle's "god" does not closely resemble the God of Judaism or Christianity. Judeo-Christian beliefs look to God as the "creator" of the universe. Aristotle did not view his god as a "creator" because one was not necessary. Being eternal, as viewed by Aristotle, the universe never had a beginning, and so it did not require being created. Aristotle's god moved the world not by force but by attraction. Just as the allure of candy might draw us into a store, so the unmoved mover drew the heavenly bodies unto motion. Thus, Aristotle found it necessary to assume that the heavenly bodies possessed some sort of innate intelligence (Adler, 1978).

Aristotle's reasoning that lead him to affirm the existence of the perfect being that he called god, or the unmoved mover, would later provide a model for theologians in their attempts to prove the existence of God—the God of Genesis.

Schooling and the Liberal Arts

In Book VIII of *Politics*, he put forward his educational theory. Following the conventional Greek distinction between "free men" and "servile men," or slaves,

Aristotle designated the liberal arts as those studies that liberate man by enlarging and expanding his choices.

Aristotle considered reading and writing, gymnastic exercises, music, and drawing as the customary branches of education. About a truly liberal education Aristotle stated, "Nature requires that we should be able, not only to work well, but to use leisure well" (Meyer, 1975, p. 38).

During the period from fifteen to twenty-one, Aristotle advocated for students a curriculum that emphasized intellectual pursuits. Mathematics, including arithmetic, geometry, and astronomy, was be studied for its practical and theoretical consequences, along with such humanistic subjects as grammar, literature, poetry, rhetoric, ethics, and politics. Upon reaching twenty-one, the student was to pursue the more theoretical and speculative studies such as physics, cosmology, biology, psychology, logic, and metaphysics (Gutek, 1972).

Logic and Rhetoric

When we hear Aristotle's name, we often think first of "Aristotelian logic." Other refined and modified systems of logic have been developed since Aristotle's day, but he laid the foundation of formal logic. Aristotle is also well known for his writings on Rhetoric. He not only influenced philosophers from the peripatetic tradition, but also such famous Roman teachers of rhetoric as Cicero and Quintilian.

The Philosopher of Common Sense

In the twelfth and thirteenth centuries, Aristotle's philosophy was re-introduced to the Western world by way of Mohammedan scholars. Scholastics such as Thomas Aquinas developed intellectual rationale for Christian theology based on the premises of Aristotelian philosophy. Aristotle's philosophy also became a basic study in the medieval universities. His metaphysics has remained an integral part of Catholic Christianity's philosophic rationale, while such modern Aristotelians as Robert Hutchins and Mortimer Adler made his realism an important cornerstone in their philosophies of education.

Life of Isocrates

Isocrates, famous for his work as a rhetorician, was born in 436 B.C., just five years before the commencement of the Peloponnesian War. His father was an

Athenian citizen named Theodorus, who was a well-to-do member of the middle class. By trade he was a manufacturer of flutes.

Tradition has it that Isocrates openly mourned in the streets following the execution of Socrates. Some have speculated that the following passage insinuates that Isocrates was at one time a pupil of Socrates. How close he actually was to Socrates is difficult to determine, but Socrates did mention him in Plato's Phaedrus:

> Isocrates is still, Phaedrus, but I do not mind telling you the future I prophesy for him. It seems to me that his natural powers give him superiority over anything that Lysias has achieved in literature, and also that in point of character he is of a nobler composition. (Plato, *Phaedrus*, 279

His School and Its Influence on Classical Education

Around the year 393 B.C., several years before Plato's famous academy was formed, Isocrates opened a school specifically for developing a liberal education, the first of its kind in Europe. His goal for students was to prepare them for careers of leadership in various cities of the Greek world. However, he hoped his best students would become teachers like himself (Marrou, 1956).

His school was significantly different from the schools of the other sophists; unlike other sophists he did not travel. He required students to come to him and to stay for an extended period of time, which gave his school stability.

To judge from what he says in *Antidosis* (287-290), he also took a personal interest in the students and their development of self-discipline, which as far as we know the sophists had not done. Finally, his school had clearly stated goals and a consistent curriculum that he maintained for over fifty years (Kennedy, 1999). How fortunate we would be if this prescribed curriculum were still extant!

While some sophists continued to emphasize civic virtue and wisdom, others sought fame and fortune by promising their students personal success. Isocrates reacted strongly against this educational confusion. In his speech, *Against the Sophists*, he attacked teachers who claimed to be able to teach virtue and also opposed those who taught rhetoric as a mechanical formula based on the mastery of a few tricks of the trade. In *Antidosis*, Isocrates wrote in defense of his own program of educational reform.

Isocrates' students enrolled in his school for a period of three to four years, during which they studied rhetorical theory, heard model orations and sample discourses, and practiced intensive declamation. To develop men of broad and liberal outlook, Isocrates also included the study of politics, ethics, and history. Ethical and political studies were intimately related and referred to the practical application of the codes of right conduct toward the gods, parents, children, friends, enemies, and society. History was both an ethical and practical subject in that it was the source of examples to be used as evidence in support of argument. He wrote, "If you are mindful of the past, you will plan better for the future" (*Ad Nicocles*, 35).

Above all, the teacher was of crucial importance in Isocrates' method of rhetorical education. As a model, the teacher had to be capable of influencing his pupils through his knowledge, skills, manners, and ethical conduct. Because of certain personal deficiencies, Isocrates did not deliver his set speeches himself; he published them.

He is supposed to have had a typical enrollment of approximately 100 students. However, he usually only had five or six students with him at a given time. With these small numbers, he became very influential with his students through genuine teaching. Thus, they thought of themselves as his disciples (Marrou, 1956).

Subject Areas

He advised his pupils to spend some time with the subject of mathematics, which he praised, like Plato, for its formative value. "Being abstract and difficult, it is a subject that accustoms the mind to sustained effort, gives it exercise and sharpens it" (*Antidosis*, 265-268).

He added another subject, which he called "Eristics"—the art of debate as taught by means of the dialogue, and which may be regarded as dialectics, or, in more general terms, philosophy. Dialectics, which for Plato was the crowning-point of the highest culture, was here relegated contemptuously to the level of a mere secondary subject.

He helped make rhetoric a central subject in the educational system of the Greek and Roman world and thus of many later centuries as well, and he established oratory as a literary form. Marrou claimed the following:

> On the whole it was Isocrates, not Plato, who educated fourth century Greece and subsequently the Hellenistic and Roman worlds; it was from Isocrates that, 'as from a Trojan horse,' there emerged all those teachers and men of culture, noble idealists, simple moralists, lovers of fine phrases, all those fluent voluble speakers, to whom classical antiquity owed both the qualities and the defects of its main cultural tradition. (1956, p. 120)

He continued by writing:

> It is to Isocrates, more than to any other person, that the honor and responsibility belong of having inspired in our Western traditional education a predominantly literary tone. Indeed as we endeavour to reconstruct the figure of this old Athenian teacher we shall all find a kind of profile emerging of one or other of our old high-school professors, the man to whom we owe so much, sometimes all that we essentially are, and of whom we have such touching memories, even if these are sometimes tinged with irony. (Marrou, p. 120)

The Life of Quintilian

Quintilian, a famous rhetorician, was born about A.D. 35 in Calagurris, a province of Spain. When he was about sixteen years old, he was sent to Rome for training in the art of rhetoric. Quintilian returned to Calagurris when he was about twenty-five.

He undoubtedly achieved prominence as a teacher and pleader back in Calagurris, for he was among those invited to go to Rome at the end of A.D. 68 with Galba, the governor of Spain, who soon became emperor of Rome in January of 69. Back in Rome, Quintilian's teaching soon attracted attention. Among his better known cases is that of the Jewish Queen Berenice, before whom Saint Paul appeared in Caesarea before going to Rome.

In A.D. 72, just four years after returning to Rome with Galba, Quintilian was included among the rhetoricians who were given an annual subsidy by the Emperor Vespasian. He rapidly attained preeminence among Roman teachers.

The peak of public recognition as a teacher came in A.D. 88, just two years prior to his retirement, when he was placed in charge of the "first public school of Rome" with an annual salary of 100,000 sesterces paid from public funds. Murphy estimated that today the amount might be equivalent to a quarter-million dollars (Murphy, 1987, xi).

It was during his retirement that he wrote his major work, the *Institutio oratoria*, or *On the Education of the Orator*. Quintilian himself informed us in the preface that he retired from teaching to secure "rest from my labors, which for twenty years I had devoted to the instruction of youth" (1987, preface, 1).

Quintilian's life was successful but not without grief. During his retirement years, his young wife died and soon after his five-year old son passed away also. In the poignant opening of Book VI of the *Institutio oratoria*, he shared his grief. He had hoped to present the completed book to his second son Quintilian. Tragically his ten year-old son died, leaving his father alone to continue his great work, now for the "studious youth" of Rome to whom he commended the book in the final paragraph of Book XII.

Institutio oratoria (On the Education of the Orator)

We are fortunate to have the entire text of *Institutio oratoria*. From it we learn the approach to education that was common in Rome by the first century AD. Quintilian's lasting theories of education were firmly based on the Greek writings of Isocrates, and greatly influenced the education of medieval students.

The *Institutio* demonstrated that the trivium studies were still the three chief tools of formal education. This comprehensive text allowed educators throughout antiquity to design their own curricula. Thus, the trivium became the common paradigm for education throughout the Western world.

Quintilian's unique gift to the educational world was that he took the time to elaborate on the details and the importance of the grammar and dialectic stages of the trivium, along with the rhetoric. His rhetorical predecessors, such as Aristotle and Isocrates, simply assumed that their readers would already be fully aware of these stages, and to address them in detail would simply be unnecessary and redundant.

The *Institutio* was divided into twelve books, with the first two books specifically devoted to what we would call today the pre-school, primary, and secondary levels of schooling. In book 3, he discussed the origin of the art of rhetoric and its different branches. Book 4 described the different parts of a speech, while in book 5 he elaborated on proofs and enthymemes. Book 6 explored the emotions involved with rhetoric, and book 7 dealt with arrangement. In books 8 and 9, Quintilian concentrated on the various uses of style, and book 10 prescribed necessary reading and writing skills. In book 11, he concentrated on memory and delivery, while the last book presented his views on what a perfect rhetorician is, and what happened when a rhetorician retired.

Like other rhetoricians before him, Quintilian thus covered the five ancient elements or parts of rhetoric:

1. *Invention* deals with the discovery of materials for the speech.

2. *Arrangement* treats the sequence or order of their appearance in the speech.

3. *Elocution*, or style, deals with the matter of wording, including such factors as vocal rhythm and rhetorical figures and tropes.

4. *Memory* deals with both natural and artificial means of recall.

5.   *Delivery* includes such external aspects as gesture, facial expression, and control of the voice.

Stages of Learning

Quintilian recognized that there are significant stages of human development that must impact our educational methodology. According to Quintilian, the years from birth to age seven are crucial for establishing the right patterns and dispositions for later education. Quintilian was concerned that parents had neglected their duties by delegating childcare to slaves. Thus, it was extremely important that all those associated with rearing children be admonished to use correct speech and pronunciation. During the latter part of this period, the child began learning to read and write the languages that he already spoke. (Quintilian, 1, 1, 14-20).

Gutek summarized the remaining years of formal instruction. The period from age seven to fourteen was when the child first formed clear ideas and further developed memory skills. The literator (reading and writing teacher) was to be of good character and be able to make learning attractive to the student. Quintilian desired that the teacher exude kindness, understanding, and refrain from using corporal punishment.

From fourteen to seventeen, the student was to study liberal arts. Greek and Latin grammars were to be studied concurrently, which included the study of Greek and Roman literatures. In addition to grammar, the student studied music, geometry, astronomy, and gymnastics. Following a thorough study of these subjects, the student was allowed to progress to the study of formal rhetoric. Interestingly, the rate of progress depended on the skills and gifts of the student. Social promotion was not accepted, with instruction geared to the student's abilities.

Quintilian recommended that rhetorical study seek to produce a man of broad culture who was willing to serve his country. The orator was not to specialize in any of the liberal arts but was to continue studying poetry, drama, prose, history, law, philosophy, and rhetoric (Gutek, 1972).

Quintilian's Impact on Classical Education

This section contains several quotes from the *Institutio* that exemplify what Quintilian considered to be acceptable practices in classical education. The reader will note that educators are still struggling today with many of these same topics. My hope is that these quotes will foster interesting discussions among readers of this book. (The first number represents the book number, the second the chapter and section.)

Character of Teachers

Let the orator, therefore, be such a man as may be called truly wise, not blameless in morals only (for that, in my opinion, though some disagree with me, is not enough), but accomplished also in science, and in every qualification for speaking—a character such as, perhaps, no man ever was. (Preface, sec. 18)

Methodology

Let him be plain in his mode of teaching, and patient of labor, but rather diligent in exacting tasks than fond of giving them of excessive length. Let him reply readily to those who put questions to him, and question of his own accord those who do not. (2, 2.5)

Teacher- or Student-Centered?

But the master ought not to speak to suit the taste of the pupils, but the pupils to suit that of the master. (2, 2.13)

Correction

In amending what requires correction, let him not be harsh, and, least of all, not reproachful; for that very circumstance, that some tutors blame students as if they hated them, deters many young men from their proposed course of study.... How much more readily we imitate those whom we like can scarcely be expressed. (2, 2.6)

Praise

Care and toil may well appear superfluous, when praise is ready for whatever the pupils have produced. (2, 2.10)

They are inclined if they receive but little praise from the master, to form an ill opinion of him. (2, 2.13)

Writing Process

We must write, therefore, as carefully, and as much, as we can; for as the ground, by being dug to a great depth, becomes more fitted for fructifying and nourishing seeds. (10, 3.2)

A different fault is that of those who wish, first of all, to run through their subject with as rapid a pen as possible, producing what they call a rough copy.... It will be better, therefore, to use care at first, and so to from our work from the beginning that we may have merely to polish it and not mold it anew. (10, 3.17-18)

Speaking

What profit does much writing, constant reading, and a long period of life spent in study, bring us, if there remains with us the same difficulty in speaking that we felt at first? (10, 7.4)

No portion even of our common conversation should ever be careless; and that whatever we say, and wherever we say it, should be as far as possible excellent in its kind. (10, 7.28)

Class Size

Every eminent teacher delights in a large concourse of pupils, and thinks himself worthy of a still numerous auditory. (1, 2.9)

Yet I would not wish a boy to be sent to place where he will be neglected. Nor should a good master encumber himself with a greater number of scholars than he can manage. (1, 2.15)

Memorization

The chief symptom of ability in children is memory, of which the excellence is twofold: to receive with ease and to retain with fidelity. The next symptom is imitation; for that is an indication of a teachable disposition. (1, 3.1)

Ideal Student

Let the boy be given to me, whom praise stimulates, whom honor delights, who weeps when he is unsuccessful. (1, 3.7)

Play and Relaxation

Yet some relaxation is to be allowed to all, not only because there is nothing that can bear perpetual labor, but because application to learning depends on the will, which cannot be forced. (1, 3.8)

It will be necessary, above all things, to take care, lest the child should conceive a dislike to the application which he cannot yet love, and continue to dread the bitterness which he has once tasted, even beyond the years of infancy. Let his instruction be an amusement to him. (1, 1.20)

Discipline

But that boys should suffer corporal punishment, though it be an accepted custom and Chrysippus makes no objection to it, I by no means approve; first, because it is a disgrace, and a punishment for slaves. (1, 3.14)

Reading Comprehension

Reading remains to be considered. Only practice can teach how a boy may know when to take breath, where to divide a verse, where the sense is concluded, where it begins, when the voice is to be raised or lowered.... There is but one direction, therefore, which I have to give in this part of my work namely, so that he may be able to do all this successfully, let him understand what he reads. (1, 8.1-2)

Rhetoric in the Grammar

Let us add, however, to the business of the grammarian, some rudiments of the art of speaking, in which they may initiate their pupils who are still too young for the teacher of rhetoric.

Paraphrasing

Let them learn, too, to take to pieces the verses of the poets, and then to express them in different words; and afterward to represent them, somewhat boldly, in a paraphrase, in which it is allowable to abbreviate or embellish certain parts.... He who shall successfully perform this exercise, which is difficult even for accomplished professors, will be able to learn anything. (1, 9.1)

Mathematics

Order, in the first place, is necessary in geometry, and is it not also necessary in eloquence? Geometry proves what follows from what precedes, what is unknown from what is known, and do we not draw similar conclusions in speaking? Does not the well-known mode of deduction from a number of proposed questions consist almost wholly in syllogisms? (1, 10.37)

Phonics

It will be best for children, therefore, to be taught the appearances and names of the letters at once, as they are taught those of men. But that which is hurtful with regard to letters, will be no impediment with regard to syllables. I do not disapprove, however, the practice, which is well known, of giving children, for the sake of stimulating them to learn, ivory figures of letters to play with, or whatever else can be invented, in which that infantile age may take delight, and which may be pleasing to handle, look at, or name. (1, 1.26)

Importance of Grammar Teachers

We are giving small instructions, while professing to educate an orator. But even studies have their infancy; and as the rearing of the very strongest bodies commenced with milk and the cradle, so he, who was to be the most eloquent of men, once uttered cries, tried to speak at first with a stuttering voice, and hesitated at the shapes of the letters. (1, 1.21)

For myself, I consider that nothing is unnecessary to the art of oratory, without which it must be confessed that an orator cannot be formed, and that there is no possibility of arriving at the summit in any subject without previous initiatory efforts: therefore, I shall not shrink from stooping to those lesser matters, the neglect of which leaves no place for greater, and shall proceed to regulate the studies of the orator from his infancy, just as if he were entrusted to me to be brought up. (Preface, section 5)

The grammarian has also need of no small portion of eloquence, that he may speak aptly and fluently on each of those subjects, which are here mentioned. Those, therefore, are not to be heeded who deride this science as trifling and empty; for unless it lays a sure foundation for the future orator, what-ever superstructure you raise will surely fall. It is an art which is necessary to the young, pleasing to the old, and an agreeable companion in retirement. (1, 4.5)

Imitation of the Master

From these authors, and others worthy to be read, must be acquired a stock of words, a variety of figures, and the art of composition. Our minds must be directed to the imitation of all their excellences, for it cannot be doubted that a great portion of art consists in imitation—for even though to invent was first in order of time and holds the first place in merit, it is nevertheless advantageous to copy what has been invented with success. (10, 2.1)

Importance of Music

Nor can anyone doubt that men eminently renowned for wisdom have been cultivators of music, when Pythagoras and those who followed him spread abroad the notions, which they doubtless received from antiquity, that the world itself was constructed in conformity with the laws of music, which the lyre afterward imitated. (1, 10.12)

For Plato thought music necessary for a man who would be qualified for engaging in government, and whom the Greeks call "statesmen." (1, 10.15)

Influence Throughout the Centuries

According to Murphy, the writings of Quintilian have had a dramatic impact on education since their advent. In the Christian realm, Origen, Ambrose, Jerome, and Saint Augustine were all trained to some extent by Quintilian's program. In medieval times, Quintilian influenced the writings of Isidore of Seville, Cassiodorus, Alcuin, and John of Salisbury. Martin Luther declared that Quintilian was his favorite authority on education. In the United States, John Quincy Adams, who held the first Boylston Chair of Rhetoric at Harvard in 1806, lectured extensively on Quintilian (Murphy, 1987).

The Life of Saint Augustine

Augustine was born at Thagaste, near Hippo, in what is now Algeria, on November 13, 354. Although respectable, his family was not rich. His father, Patricius, was a middle class farmer and a town councilor with the duty of collecting taxes. His father was a pagan but his mother, Monica, was a devout Christian. However, one year before his death, Patricius did accept Christ and became a Christian. Apparently Augustine was not close to his father, mentioning his father's death only once in his vast array of writings (Piper, 2000).

Much of what we know of the life of Augustine came to us from Augustine himself in his somewhat autobiographical work entitled *Confessions*. Here he recorded for us the story of his life until his dramatic conversion and the death of his mother soon thereafter.

In his *Confessions,* he acknowledged that he initially hated school. Augustine attended grammar school in Madaura, a neighboring city. Later he would continue his education in Carthage.

> Yet even before my testing time as a young man, even in my childhood, I resisted education and despised those pressing it upon me, though they pressed anyway, and good was done me though I myself did not good.

> Why I loathed Greek lessons, when I was plunged into them at an early age, I have not to this day been able to fathom. I took fondly to Latin, not indeed from my first tutors but from those called teachers of literature. The basic reading, writing, and numbering in Latin I considered as dull and irksome as any aspect of my Greek lessons—the explanation of which must be sin. (*Confessions*, 1.20)

Despite the use of threats and the flogging system, he refused to learn Greek. However, he did express appreciation for the gifts of reading and writing.

> Actually, the basic lessons were the more valuable ones, just because they went by rule, letting me acquire and retain the ability I still hold to read any book I come across, or to write exactly what I want to say. (*Confessions*, 1.20)

By the time he reached the age of sixteen, Augustine related, he and his friends roamed the streets looking for trouble after dusk, and saved their worst pranks until after midnight (*Confessions*, 2.9).

When Augustine completed his studies in Madaura, he was to continue his education through the study of rhetoric in the city of Carthage. Unfortunately, his father no longer had enough money to support such studies, so he spent his sixteenth year at home. He complimented his father for how diligent he was in trying to raise funds for his son's education, but Augustine lamented how little concern his father showed for his proper upbringing. His father's priority was that Augustine would become gifted in rhetoric.

Concerning his eventual three years of education in Carthage, Augustine told us that he was an outstanding student, being at the top of his class. However, he was discouraged by the inappropriate behavior exhibited by his classmates. He was saddened especially by how they treated the incoming students (*Confessions*, 2.5-2.6).

But according to Piper (2000), his own lifestyle was less than exemplary. During this time, he took a mistress and had a son with her named Adeodatus. He would continue to live with her for fifteen years. Sadly, Augustine mentioned her often in his *Confessions* but never refers to her by name.

While a student in Carthage, he became enamored with the writings of Cicero, whose words created within him a strong desire to study philosophy. He also longed to develop a relationship with the God of his youth.

> In the ordinary course of study, I fell upon a certain book of, whose speech almost all admire, not so his heart. This book of his contains an exhortation to philosophy, and is called *Hortensius*. But this book altered my affections, and turned my prayers to Thyself, O Lord; and made me have other purposes and desires. Every vain hope at once became worthless to me; and I longed with an incredibly burning desire for an immortality of wisdom, and began now to arise, that I might return to thee. (*Confessions*, 3.7)

From Cicero, he embraced the idea to seek wisdom wherever it might be found. However, he was greatly disappointed that Cicero never mentioned the God of Christianity. Thus, he turned to the scriptures for wisdom but thought they were crude in comparison to the eloquence of Cicero's writings (Wills, 1999).

He began to explore Manicheism. Manicheism was a Christian heresy established by Mani, its founder and martyr. Christ was the second person of the trinity, or the Light, who communicated the will of the father to those on earth. The third person was Mani himself. Manicheans believed that humans contained exiled God-particles that had to be wrestled free from the enveloping power of evil. Augustine found this dilemma exemplified in his own life related to his struggle with sexual temptation (Wills, 1999).

Having completed his studies at Carthage, he returned to his hometown of Thagaste in 374 and became a teacher of rhetoric. In 376, he decided to return to Carthage, this time as a teacher, not a student (*Confessions*, 4.7).

After dealing with unruly students for a number of years in Carthage, Augustine decided to relocate once again, this time to Rome. Apparently, Augustine had become the victim of the antics that he had exhibited to his teachers in his younger years.

> My motive in going to Rome was not that the friends who urged it on me promised higher fees and a greater position of dignity, though at that time these considerations had an influence on my mind. The principal and almost sole reason was that I had heard how at Rome the young men went quietly about their studies and were kept in order by a stricter imposition of discipline.... By contrast at Carthage the license of the students is foul and uncontrolled. They impudently break in and with almost mad behavior disrupt the order which each teacher has established for his pupils' benefit. (*Confessions*, 5.14)

Augustine's mother was devastated about his plans and begged him to remain with her. Augustine deceived her by convincing her that his ship would not be leaving until morning. Monica left to visit a nearby shrine to continue praying for her son. Under the cover of darkness, he left along with his mistress and son, leaving his mother weeping for him. He recounted in *Confessions* that she did not yet know that God had a plan for his life that would bring her tremendous joy, which was his eventual conversion to Christianity (Confessions, 5.17).

Augustine arrived in Rome, deathly ill and quite certain he was going to die. In his *Confessions*, Augustine thanked God for sparing his life and his mother the grief of losing her son prior to his salvation (*Confessions*, 5.17).

Having arrived in Rome, he established a school of rhetoric in his home and his reputation began to develop. His students were better behaved than those he had taught in Africa. However, he became greatly disillusioned when some of his students banded together and sought another teacher in order to avoid paying their tuition (*Confessions*, 5.22).

Upon hearing that a position as the teacher of rhetoric in Milan was available, he applied for the post and was appointed. Milan had recently become the administrative capital of the Roman Empire, but the most influential figure in the city may have been Bishop Ambrose, who treated Augustine with kindness and was very influential in his coming to know Christ (*Confessions*, 5.23).

Augustine told us that approximately a year after his arrival in Milan, his mother, Monica, arrived to live with him. Monica was able to convince Augustine that it was time for him to find a proper wife. Through the efforts of his mother, arrangements were made for Augustine to become engaged. His bride-to-be was probably only ten years old, as Augustine told us that he was required to wait two years before he could legally marry her (*Confessions*, 6.24). According to Wills (1999), the legal age of marriage under Roman law was 12.

As a strong admirer of Augustine, I find his decision to force his mistress to return to Africa alone after a 15-year relationship difficult to understand.

> Since she was an obstacle to my marriage, the woman I had lived with for so long was torn out of my side. My heart, to which she had been grafted, was lacerated, wounded, shedding blood (*Confessions*, 6.25).

Wills speculated that Augustine believed that as a philosopher he would be more effective if he could remain celibate. Being unable to do so with his long-time mistress, Wills (1999) speculated that he may have hoped that having such a young bride would enable him to do so.

Augustine's Conversion

On the day of his conversion, he was in a garden with his friend Alypius. August-ine left him for a time and sat by himself for a time of contemplation. He heard children in the background chanting. In his *Confessions,* he related his joyful story:

> As I was saying this and weeping in the bitter agony of my heart, suddenly I heard a voice from the nearby house chanting as if it might be a boy or girl (I do not know which), saying and repeating over and over again 'Pick up and read, pick up and read.' At once my countenance changed, and I began to think intently whether there might be some sort of children's game in which such a chant is used. But I could not remember having heard of one. I checked the flood of tears and stood up. I interpreted it solely as a divine command to me to open the book and read the first chapter I might find…. So I hurried back to the place where Alypius was sitting. There I had put down the book of the apostle when I got up. I seized it, opened it and in silence read the first passage on which my eyes lit: 'Not in riots and drunken parties, not in eroti-cism and indecencies, not in strife and rivalry, but put on the Lord Jesus Christ and make no provision for the flesh in its lusts' (Romans 13: 13-14).
>
> I neither wished nor needed to read further. At once, with the last words of this sentence, it was as if a light of relief from all anxiety flooded into my heart. All the shadows of doubt were dispelled. (*Confessions,* 8.29)

Alypius and Augustine went immediately to Augustine's mother to tell her the good news. Augustine also soon decided that he no longer needed to seek the wife that might give him financial success, as this was no longer of importance to him (*Confessions,* 8.3).

Following his conversion in 386, Augustine sought a complete change in life-style. He took a leave of absence from his court position because of poor health and moved to a villa in Cassiciacum with several friends and his stenographers from Milan. In 387, he returned to Milan and was baptized, along with his son, by Bishop Ambrose.

Augustine soon decided to return to Africa, but while in route his mother died. So at the age of thirty-five, he returned to Thagaste and formed a small monastery with several of his friends. Soon thereafter, tragedy would again strike. This time his son, Adeodatus, died at the age of sixteen. One can only speculate whether his mother was able to be with him when he passed away (*Confessions,* 9.29).

In 390, Augustine, while visiting the nearby city of Hippo, found himself forced into the priesthood by the pleas of the local church. In 395, upon the death of Bishop Valerius, Augustine assumed the post of bishop, an office he would hold until his death thirty-four years later (Piper, 1999).

Saint Augustine's Impact on Classical Education

Augustine did not share Tertullian's fear of classical education. He drew from classical literature as well as Christian sources in developing what is considered the first full-blown theory of Christian education (Elias, 2002).

Howie stated that St. Augustine's most valuable contributions to the understanding of education stem from his Christian Platonism. In the introduction to his book *St. Augustine on Education*, Howie provided a summation of Augustine's union of philosophy and Christian revelation under three headings:

1.   The Motivation of Learning

2.   Communication between Teacher and Pupil

3.   The Content of the Christian Curriculum. (1969, p. 10)

The Motivation of Learning

Plato viewed education as a reaching out of the soul toward a distant, impersonal source of knowledge known as "the Good" or "the One." Augustine understood education within the context of a personal relationship between God, the author of truth, and man whom he had created. Thus, the purpose of all educational effort is the understanding of the nature of God and his creation.

Within this framework, St. Augustine developed his view on the motivation of learning. Learning always has a clear purpose in view; the mind must be stimulated to possess some particular thought or idea. If a thing is to be desired, the learner must have faith that it really exists and can be known. In the case of the objects of intellectual knowledge, faith is the precondition of understanding (Howie, 1969).

Thus, Augustine's theory of Christian education agrees well with the basic educational concept that new learning is built on existing experience, and that we learn best when we move from the known to the unknown.

According to Augustine, the desire to learn can only be kindled by a sensitive and caring teacher who reflected the love of God to his or her students. The teacher also had a responsibility to "love" the subjects he or she taught, and to be aware that God is the source of all truth (Howie, 1969).

Augustine also advocated expressing love to the students based on their individual needs and temperaments. "The same medicine is not to be given to all, although to all the same love is due—to some love is gentle, to others severe, an enemy to none, a mother to all" (cited in Howie, 1969, p. 15).

Communication between Teacher and Pupil

Augustine was critical of rote learning if it consisted of unthinking and meaningless repetition of words. In the *Confessions*, he was extremely critical of chanting, which he condemned as a detestable feature of his own elementary education (1.22). (Teachers who strictly adhere to the Sayers' model of the grammar stage might find Augustine's comment disturbing.)

Augustine also rejected the view that the teacher is in any real sense the cause of learning. He insisted that the cause of learning is set in motion by the effort of the learner's free will (Howie, 1969).

According to Augustine, the teacher could be very helpful in the learning process, but was not essential. What was necessary was for the learner to be closely involved with the subject matter (Howie, 1969)).

The learner is his own teacher. The teacher in the classroom, whom Augustine called "the external teacher," may ask questions or display objects to stimulate the learner's interest, but in the final analysis the learner is most responsible for the learning process (Howie, 1969, pp. 15-16).

In *The Teacher*, Augustine provided further clarification to this idea of learning. He called the classroom teacher, or external teacher, the *magister exterior*. The internal teacher, or *magister interior,* is not the student but is the Word of God, which illuminates the eternal truths (sections 38-40).

In this process of attaining truth, Saint Augustine replaced Plato's doctrine of learning as "remembering" with the notion of "divine illumination" (Howie, 1969, p. 16).

Thus, the whole argument in *The Teacher* was designed to encourage a critical appraisal of the nature and function of teaching. The teacher must be careful not to confuse rote memorization with real understanding. "Who is so absurdly foolish, as to send his son to school to learn what the teacher thinks?" Augustine asked in *The Teacher* (section 45).

The purpose of formal schooling was to encourage the learner to think for himself. Thus, the teacher must challenge and help develop the learner's powers of thought (Teacher, section 45).

The Content of the Christian Curriculum

To his duties as a Christian pastor and teacher, St. Augustine brought the culture of the classical liberal arts curriculum, which he had learned as a student and teacher. He incorporated the liberal arts in a Christian theory of knowledge. He regarded them as the indispensable bases of all knowledge. He thought of the liberal arts as the proper nutriment of the soul, just as food is that of the body:

> The souls of those who have not drunk from the fountains of the liberal arts are, as it were, hungry and famished; this is a condition of sterility, what we may call a spiritual famine; the minds of such people are full of diseases, which betray their malnutrition. (as cited in Howie, 1969, p. 18)

Thus, the educational function of the liberal arts is to lead the learner to an understanding of real existence. In his treatise entitled *On Music,* he wrote:

> My desire is that, with the love of unchanging truth, they should attach themselves to the one God and Lord of all, who presides over the minds of men with no material object coming between. (as cited in Howie, 1969, p. 19)

Life of Cassiodorus

Magnus Aurelius Cassiodorus Senator was born ca. 480 at Scyllacium in southern Italy. His father, the third Cassiodorus, rose to great eminence under Odovacar, (or Odoacer) and later under the rule of Theodoric. Odovacar was a Germanic warrior who worked his way up through the ranks of the Roman army. Odovacar deposed Romulus Augustus, officially putting an end to the Western Roman Empire in 476 A.D.

Education and Public Service

Cassiodorus' own writings indicated that he received the usual instruction in philosophy and rhetoric that was given the young noble who aspired to governmental office. He served as a consiliarius, or assessor, a quaestor, and in several other political positions.

Founding of the Monastery

In 536 A.D., Cassiodorus decided to retire from public life. He now planned to spend his old age in religious meditation and commenting on the Christian Scriptures. During this time, Cassiodorus decided to found a monastery at his ancestral home of Scyllacium, between the mountains of Aspromonte and the sea. His goal was to establish a school of theology and Christian literature similar to the school at Alexandria.

Cassiodorus was determined to utilize the vast leisure of the convent for the preservation of ecclesiastical and secular learning. He made his monastery a theological school and a *scriptorium* for making multiple copies of the scripture and writings of the early church Fathers. He also had copies made of the great secular writers of antiquity. Among his other accomplishments, he divided the books of the Bible into chapters and provided summaries of the chapters at the beginning of each book.

Contributions to Classical Education

Institutiones divinarum et humanarum lectionum, or *An Introduction to Divine and Human Readings,* written for the instruction of his monks some time around 551 A.D., is undoubtedly Senator's best work. Doug Wilson in his recent book, *The Case for Classical Education* (2003), credits Cassiodorus with helping to make a liberal arts education (the quadrivium of grammar, dialectic, rhetoric, arithmetic, geometry, music, and astronomy) a standardized part of education in the Middle Ages. Cassiodorus' work of categorizing education around the seven pillars of the quadrivium was not original (Capella had done so in *The Marriage of Philology and Mercury*). However, unlike Capella, he approached the quadrivium from a Christian perspective.

As its title implies, the book is divided into two sections. In the first section entitled *Divine Letters,* he dealt primarily with biblical content, important commentators, and the various methods of understanding the Scriptures. However, he was also concerned about varied topics such as proper spelling and in what materials doctors should be well versed. Cassiodorus shared that he arrived at the specific number of 33 topics because it corresponds with the age of Christ at his death. (Please see Table 1 for the list of topics that he expounded upon in his book and the precise order in which they should be studied.)

Book two entitled *Secular Letters* contains a brief account of the seven liberal arts—grammar, rhetoric, dialectic, arithmetic, geometry, music, and astronomy. Cassiodorus based his writings on the works of numerous authors, most of whom are listed in his book.

Cassiodorus transformed the monastery into a theological school that not only preserved and produced multiple copies of the Scriptures, but also was responsible for preserving the works of many great secular writers of antiquity. Book II of the *Institutiones* also became one of the important schoolbooks of the early Middle Ages.

We can credit Cassiodorus with playing an important role in preserving the wisdom of the ages. He died at the age of ninety-five, after a long and industrious career as statesman and theological scholar.

Additional Studies

In this chapter, I have attempted to provide a brief summation regarding those educators who played a key role in the development of the trivium from the time of the great Greek philosophers to the middle ages.

By necessity many scholars were not included. For those interested specifically in the art of rhetoric and the influence of Cicero, I strongly recommend the new biography entitled, *Cicero: The Life and Times of Rome's Greatest Politician.*

The life of Boethius also makes for interesting reading. This politician and philosopher wrote his famous *Consolation of Philosophy* while imprisoned and awaiting execution. This work functioned as a textbook throughout the middle ages.

During my research I was also fascinated by the life of Peter Abelard and his famous romance with Heloise. While reading a biography recently about Carly Fiorina, the CEO of HP, I found that she has a classics background and has made numerous references to Abelard in her writings. (A short section on Abelard is included in a later chapter.)

This book would certainly be more complete with a chapter on the reformers such as Calvin and Luther, who were very committed to establishing schools.

4

The Rise of Universities

In this study of the history and development of the classical trivium, I would be remiss to omit a brief history concerning the development of the medieval university system. For it was the development of this revered institution that allowed for an amalgamation of the past 1500 years of classical thought to come to fruition in a systematic and orderly fashion. Unlike the vast majority of students today, the scholars of the medieval day came to the universities already possessing the skills of the trivium. There they had the opportunity to continue their studies through the quadrivium (astronomy, music, math, and geometry).

Universities, like cathedrals and parliaments, are a creation of the Middle Ages. The highly educated Greeks and the Romans had no universities in the sense that the word has been used for the past 900 years. Although they provided outstanding instruction in law, rhetoric, and philosophy, their methodology was not organized into the form of permanent institutions of learning. While Plato's Academy lasted over 900 years, certificates of attendance or diplomas were never awarded. Not until the twelfth and thirteenth centuries do we recognize those familiar phenomena of faculties, colleges, courses of study, examinations, commencements, and academic degrees. We owe this legacy not to Athens or Rome but to Paris and Bologna.

The academic gild that formed in Paris and Bologna gave us our first and our best definition of a university, a society of masters and scholars. Historically, the word university has no connection with the universe or the universality of learning; it denotes only the totality of a group, whether of barbers, carpenters, or students. The term is derived from the Latin term for union, *universitas*. Initially, Bologna's students formed a gild and virtually controlled the university. Eventually, the professors also formed a gild and were able to determine admission standards, so that no student could enter, save by the gild's consent.

41

The first section of this chapter deals with the history of early medieval universities, the second with university instruction, and the third with short biographies of two famous and influential professors.

As Graves (1910) reminded us, the beginnings of the oldest universities are obscure and uncertain, so in this chapter I must be content to restrict my comments to very generalized statements.

Origins of the Medieval University

The occasion for the rise of universities was a great revival of learning, sometimes known as the renaissance of the twelfth century. By the twelfth century, enrollment at certain cathedral schools had grown so large that the existing patterns of organization were inadequate to accommodate the large numbers of students. Related events such as the crusades, the revival of commerce, and Western contacts with Arabic scholarship contributed directly to the advent of the university system. Between 1100 and 1200, western Europe received a great influx of new knowledge from the Arab scholars of Spain. These included the works of Aristotle, Euclid, Ptolemy, and the Greek physicians, the new arithmetic, and those texts of the Roman law. According to Gutek (1972), this new knowledge created a need for an educational institution that would take students beyond what was being taught in the cathedral and monastery schools and create the learned professions.

During this time, certain teachers such as Abelard, Duns Scotus, and Thomas Aquinas, were so acclaimed that thousands of students came to hear them lecture. The attraction that these famous scholars received also contributed to the rise of the universities. Theological exploration was a major interest of the medieval scholastics, especially at the University of Paris, where Thomas Aquinas and other scholars sought to reconcile the rediscovered Greek rationalism of Aristotle with the revealed scriptural of the Christian faith.

According to Gutek, an examination of the origins of the medieval university revealed certain general trends:

1.   Many of the universities evolved from and frequently absorbed the *studia generalia* of the older cathedral schools.

2.   The general stimulus emanating from the revival of learning contributed to the support and growth of the universities.

3.   The introduction of new learning and the rediscovery of classical Greek rationalism created problems of synthesis for the scholastics who tried to

reconcile these new intellectual sources with the corpus of Christian doctrine.

4. Revived commercial and city life produced a mobile and cosmopolitan body of scholars and students who populated the universities.

5. The faculties and students of the universities followed the examples of the existing guilds and assumed the powers of self-government, establishing internal structures and enacting internal regulations.

6. The medieval universities established specialized schools for one or more of the major professional studies of law, medicine, and theology. (1972, p. 85)

The Early Universities

University of Salerno

The oldest of the universities was that at Salerno, near Naples. This organization seems to have been simply a school of medicine, and may owe its origin primarily to the survival of the old Greek medical works in this part of the peninsula.

By the middle of the eleventh century, the revival of medicine was well under way and Salerno was known as the leading place for medical study. According to Graves (1910), a tremendous asset to the school occurred with the arrival of a converted Jew called Constantinus Africanus. He had wandered through India, Babylonia, and Egypt, and everywhere he traveled he studied medicine. He had fled to Salerno from Carthage, and during the second half of the eleventh century collected and translated Hippocrates and numerous other Greek and Arabic medical authorities. Salerno's reputation was also greatly elevated by the visit of Robert, Duke of Normandy, in 1099, who came to seek treatment for a wound suffered during the first Crusade. His returning knights spread the fame of the school to all parts of Europe. Salerno, however, was never chartered as a regular university, and did not receive any official recognition until 1231. At that time, Frederick II recognized the medical program but it never became a model for other universities. By the 14th century, it faced a permanent decline.

University of Bologna

Early in the twelfth century, Bologna became a preeminent university. The city, which had been known for its school of liberal arts, was now made famous by the lectures upon law by Irnerius. For the first time, the entire *Corpus Juris Civilis*

(*Body of Civil Law*), the collected works of Roman law made by prominent jurists in the sixth century by order of the emperor Justinian, was collected and critically discussed.

But Bologna was also destined to become the seat for the study of canon law. A monk named Gratian was driven to endow the Church with a code no less organized than the *Corpus Juris Civilis*. Gratian undertook in 1142 to organize all edicts, legislation, and statements of popes, councils, Church fathers, and Christian emperors in a suitable textbook. This work became known as the *Decretum Gratiani* (The Decree of Gratian). It became the authority upon the subject, and Gratian competed with Irnerius for the level of impact upon the reputation of Bologna. Canon law was now made a separate study from theology, and attracted a large number of students (Graves, 1910).

The school at Bologna was chartered as a university by Frederick Barbarossa in 1158, and by the beginning of the thirteenth century it is estimated that there were about five thousand students in attendance.

Already we recognize at Bologna the standard academic degrees as well as the university organization and well-known officials like the rector. Other subjects of study appeared in the course of time (arts, medicine, and theology), but Bologna was preeminently, a school of civil law, and as such, it became the model of university organization for Italy, Spain, and southern France.

University of Paris

Of all the universities north of the Alps, the first was developed in Paris, which became the most famous of all medieval universities. This university was an offshoot of the cathedral school of Notre Dame, which had an excellent reputation due to the leadership of William of Champeaux. But in Paris, the academic movement was impacted most by the brilliant Abelard, who taught in Paris between 1108 and 1139.

In 1117, Abelard succeeded to the position from which he had driven William following William's defeat by Abelard in a famous debate. According to Graves (1910), Abelard drew thousands of students to Paris from all nations. It is estimated that a pope, nineteen cardinals, and more than fifty bishops and archbishops were at one time among his pupils. He lectured in the areas of dialectic and theology, and strongly encouraged free discussion and gave liberation to the use of reason.

Thus, Abelard became the progenitor of the University of Paris, but it was not fully organized until almost a generation after his death when the university was sanctioned by King Louis VII in 1180. Eighteen years later the university's privileges substantially increased by the endorsement of Pope Celestine III. Abelard's successor was his pupil, Peter the Lombard, who became the author of the great medieval textbook upon theology entitled *Sententia.*

At Bologna the students, who were usually mature men, had entire charge of the government of the university. They selected the masters and determined the fees, length of term, and time of beginning. However, in Paris initially the students were younger and the government was in the hands of the masters. Consequently, new universities in the North were known as master-universities, while those in the South were called student-universities (Haskins, 1923).

When Paris ceased to be a cathedral school and became a university, no one can say, although it was certainly before the end of the twelfth century. Officially, the University of Paris has chosen 1200, the year of its first royal charter. In that year, after certain students had been killed in a "town and gown" altercation, King Philip Augustus issued a formal privilege that recognized the exemption of the students and their servants from lay jurisdiction, thus creating that special position of students before the court.

Paris was preeminent in the Middle Ages as a school of theology, and theology was considered to be the supreme subject of medieval study. According to an old saying, "The Italians have the Papacy, the Germans have the Empire, and the French have Learning" (cited in Haskins, 1923, p. 28). Paris was to become the source and the model for many northern universities. (By the end of the Middle Ages, at least eighty universities had been founded in different parts of Europe.)

Oxford University

In England, Oxford began in the second half of the twelfth, and Cambridge at the beginning of the thirteenth century, although their first recognition by charter cannot easily be determined. The Oxford University Web presents this brief history of the development of the university:

> Oxford is an unique and historic institution. As the oldest English-speaking university in the world, it can lay claim to nine centuries of continuous existence. There is no clear date of foundation, but teaching existed at Oxford in some form in 1096 and developed rapidly from 1167, when Henry II banned English students from attending the University of Paris.
>
> In 1188, the historian, Gerald of Wales, gave a public reading to the assembled Oxford dons and in 1190 the arrival of Emo of Friesland, the first known overseas student, set in train the University's tradition of international scholarly links. By 1201, the University was headed by a magister scolarum Oxo-

nie, on whom the title of Chancellor was conferred in 1214, and in 1231 the masters were recognized as a universitas or corporation.

In the 13th century, rioting between town and gown (townspeople and students) hastened the establishment of primitive halls of residence. These were succeeded by the first of Oxford's colleges, which began as medieval 'halls of residence' or endowed houses under the supervision of a Master. University, Balliol and Merton Colleges, established between 1249 and 1264, are the oldest.

Less than a century later, Oxford had achieved eminence above every other seat of learning, and won the praises of popes, kings and sages by virtue of its antiquity, curriculum, doctrine and privileges. In 1355, Edward III paid tribute to the University for its invaluable contribution to learning; he also commented on the services rendered to the state by distinguished Oxford graduates.

(http://www.ox.ac.uk/aboutoxford/history.shtml).

Cambridge University

The following brief history of Cambridge University is presented on the university's website.

When we first come across Cambridge in written records, it was already a considerable town. The bridge across the River Cam or Granta, from which the town took its name, had existed since at least 875. The town was an important trading centre before the Domesday survey was compiled in 1086, by which time a castle stood on the rising ground to the north of the bridge, and there were already substantial commercial and residential properties as well as several churches in the main settlement which lay south of the bridge. Within the town, or very close to it, there were a number of other religious institutions. There had been canons in the Church of St Giles below the castle before 1112, when they moved to a new site across the River Cam at Barnwell, and the Convent of St Radegund had existed since 1135 on the site which eventually became Jesus College. There were also two hospitals, one reserved for lepers at Stourbridge, and a second, founded for paupers and dedicated to St John, which after 1200 occupied the site where St John's College now stands. Seventeen miles north of the town was the great Benedictine house of Ely which, after 1109, was the seat of a Bishopric.

There was thus much to bring clerks (clergymen) to the town, but traders were also attracted to it. After about 1100 they could reach Cambridge easily by the river systems which drained the whole of the East Midlands, and through Lynn and Ely they had access to the sea. Much wealth accumulated in the town, and the eleven surviving medieval parish churches and at least one handsome stone house remain as evidence of this. There were food markets before 1066, and during the twelfth century the nuns of St Radegund were allowed to set up a fair on their own land at Garlic Lane; the canons of Barnwell had a fair in June (later Midsummer Fair), and the leper hospital was granted the right to hold a fair which developed into the well-known and long-lasting Stourbridge Fair.

By 1200, Cambridge was a thriving commercial community which was also a county town and had at least one school of some distinction. Then, in 1209, scholars taking refuge from hostile townsmen in Oxford migrated to Cambridge and settled there. They were numerous enough by 1226 to have set up an organisation, represented by an official called a Chancellor, and seem to have arranged regular courses of study, taught by their own members. King Henry III took them under his protection as early as 1231 and arranged for them to be sheltered from exploitation by their landlords. At the same time he tried to ensure that they had a monopoly of teaching, by an order that only those enrolled under the tuition of a recognised master were to be allowed to remain in the town.

(www.cam.ac.uk/cambuniv/pubs/history/).

University of Prague

The first German university, that of Prague, was not instituted until 1348, but, before the close of the century, Vienna, Erfurt, Heidelberg, and Cologne had sprung up, and twice as many more appeared within the next hundred years.

Curriculum

The basis of education in the early Middle Ages consisted "of the Aristotelian idea of the educated person, 'critical' in all or almost all branches of knowledge" (Van Doren, 1991, p. 41). Instruction was based on the seven liberal arts. Three of these, grammar, rhetoric, and logic, were grouped as the trivium; the remaining four, arithmetic, geometry, astronomy, and music, made up the quadrivium. Haskins stated, "The whole conception reached the Middle Ages chiefly in the book (*The Marriage of Philogy and Mercury*) of a certain Martianus Capella, written in the early fifth century" (1923, p. 28).

According to Haskins (1923), it was a bookish age and instruction followed closely the written word.

In the monastic and cathedral schools of the earlier period the text-books were few and simple, chiefly the Latin grammars of Donatus and Priscian with some elementary reading-books, the logical manuals of Boethius, as well as his arithmetic and music, a manual of rhetoric, the most elementary propositions of geometry, and an outline of practical astronomy such as that of the Venerable Bede.

Of Greek, of course, there was none. This slender curriculum in arts was much enlarged by the renaissance of the twelfth century, which added to the store of western knowledge the astronomy of Ptolemy, the complete works of Euclid, and the Aristotelian logic, while at the same time under the head of grammar great importance was given to the study and reading of the Latin classics. This classical revival, which is noteworthy and comparatively little known, centered in such cathedral schools as Chartres and Orieans, where the spirit of a real humanism showed itself in an enthusiastic study of ancient authors and in the production of Latin verses of a really remarkable quality. Nevertheless, though brilliant, this classical movement was short-lived, crushed in its youth by the triumph of logic and the more practical studies of law and rhetoric. In the later twelfth century John of Salisbury inveighed against the logicians of his day, with their superficial knowledge of literature. In the university curriculum of the twelfth century, literary studies had quite disappeared. (pp. 38-40)

In his book *The Metalogicon*, completed in 1159, John of Salisbury argued for a greater emphasis to be placed on literature as part of the training in grammar.

Grammar is the cradle of all philosophy, and in a manner of speaking, the first nurse of the whole study of letters. It takes all of us as tender babes, newly born from nature's bosom. It nurses us in our infancy, and guides our every forward step in philosophy. With motherly care, it fosters and protects the philosopher from the start to the finish of his pursuits.... So also this branch, which teaches language, is the first of the arts to assist those who are aspiring to increase in wisdom. For it introduces wisdom both through ears and eyes by its facilitation of verbal intercourse.... One who is ignorant of grammar cannot philosophize any easier than one who lacks sight and hearing from birth can become an eminent philosopher. (chap. 13, pts. 154–161)

Haskins also shared:

The earliest university statutes, those of Paris in 1215, required the whole of Aristotle's logical works, and throughout the Middle Ages, these remain the backbone of the arts course. In a sense this is perfectly just, for logic was not only a major subject of study itself, it pervaded every other subject as a method and gave tone and character to the mediaeval mind. Syllogism, disputation, the orderly marshalling of arguments for and against specific these, these became the intellectual habit of the age in law and medicine as well as in philosophy and theology. The logic of course, was Aristotle's, and the other works of the philosopher soon followed, so that in the Paris course of 1254 we find also the *Ethics*, the *Metaphysics*, and the various treatises on natural science which had at first been forbidden to students. (1923, pp. 41-42)

The study of classical literature became confined to examples and excerpts designed to illustrate the rules of grammar. Rhetoric was also reduced to a subordinate position with the studies of the quadrivium receiving but scant attention. The arts course was mainly a course in logic and philosophy. Scientific laboratories and the study of history did not exist until long after the Middle Ages. Haskins (1923) also pointed out that, contrary to the common impression, there were relatively few students of theology in the early mediaeval universities, for a prescribed theological training for the priesthood came in only with the Counter Reformation. The requirements for admission to study theology were difficult to attain, while the curriculum consisted of a long and tedious study of the Bible and Peter Lombard's *Sentences*. In law, the basis of all instruction was inevitably the *Corpus Juris Civilis* of Justinian.

The study of medicine likewise was based on books—chiefly of Galen and Hippocrates with their Arabic translators and commentators. Haskins (1923) stated that the mediaeval universities made no contributions to medical knowledge during this time, for the study of medicine was not adaptable to their prevailing method of verbal and syllogistic dogmatism.

The course in arts led normally to the master's degree in six years, with the baccalaureate somewhere on the way. Graduation in arts was the common prerequisite for prospective theologians, lawyers, and physicians. "A sound tradition, to which the American world has given too little attention!" lamented Haskins in 1923 (p. 46).

A reading knowledge of Latin was the only academic requirement needed for admission into the arts course, the basic course of study that was the prerequisite for advanced professional studies in theology, law, and medicine. The arts included grammar, philosophy, logic, rhetoric, metaphysics, and mathematics. The time devoted to studying the arts varied from four to seven years. According to the scholastic conception of education, learning was arranged in a pyramid, or hierarchy, of studies. Beginning with the liberal arts at the base of the pyramid, the student progressed upward through philosophy and finally reached theology, the queen of medieval studies, located at the summit. Theology served to integrate the various bodies of knowledge into a pattern that conformed to the medieval theocentric conception of reality.

Pedagogy of Scholasticism

By the eleventh century, theologians had begun to seriously discuss philosophical problems related to Christian theology. Their endeavors resulted in the development of scholasticism as a methodology of inquiry, scholarship, and teaching.

Dahmus (1995) provided the following definition of scholasticism:

> As the term came to be applied, it referred more specifically to the scholar who pursued the study of logic and of metaphysics in his conviction that a knowledge of those subjects would facilitate his study of Christian theology. Scholasticism might therefore be defined as the system of thought that dominated the schools of the Middle Ages from the eleventh to the fifteenth century, which had as its objective the clarification of Christian faith with the help of reason. (p. 326)

Dahmus (1995) also referred to Anselm as the father of scholasticism:

> The scholastic whose learning, piety, and charm dispelled the misgivings and hostility of many churchmen and assured scholasticism honored reception in the church was Lanfranc's pupil, Anselm of Bec. For this, if for no other accomplishment, Anselm merits the title "father of scholasticism."...Despite his enormous debt to St. Augustine with whom his thinking is in complete harmony, Anselm is considered an unusually original thinker. The Christian should never doubt what the church taught, so argued Anselm. Yet God gave man a mind and he was expected to use it. When confronted with some problem in faith which he wished to clarify, the Christian should 'as far as he is able, to seek the reason for it. If he can understand it, let him thank God. If he cannot, let him not raise his head in opposition but bow in reverence.' (p. 327)

As an educational method, scholasticism was highly verbal and academically minded. The scholastic relied heavily upon the methodologies of lecture and disputation. Using Aristotelian logic as a structure for academic inquiry, the scholastic, using disputation, began with a carefully worded question, reviewed the authorities, and proposed a correct answer to the question posed initially; he then refuted objections that were mustered against his conclusion.

The chief instructional method, the lecture, consisted of a reading and explanation of the text under consideration together with its glosses (interpretations of specific vocabulary). Since students copied the lecture, the professor had to read the passage repeatedly and slowly enough for them to copy it. In fact, university regulations prohibited a professor from lecturing too hastily. At the end of a course, the student would thus possess a complete copy of the text, with the lecturer's explanations. The scholastics and their students investigated controversies within a framework bounded by Christian Scripture and Aristotelian logic. However, at this stage in the university's development, the scholastics tended to ignore scientific and empirical modes of inquiry.

Pedagogical Crisis: Nominalism Versus Realism

Although issues arose as to the primacy of faith or reason as a methodological authority, the scholastics generally regarded both as complementary sources of truth. By faith, the scholastic accepted the Scriptures as God's revealed Word, while also trusting that his intellect would function rationally and logically. The scholastic, reasoning deductively and syllogistically from a priori first principles, used his mind as a sure guide to God's universal truth, but did not really extensively on the direct sense experience of the eternal world.

The issue of nominalism versus realism centering on the relationship between words and the reality to which they referred, caused major controversy among the medieval scholastics.

Realists

The realists, asserting that universal ideas, or forms, exist independently and prior to individual objects, posited reality in a world of unchanging essences or forms. God, the most universal and abstract Being, is the Source of all reality. Universal concepts of goodness, justice, truth, and beauty derive from the ultimate reality and give form to individual acts of goodness and justice and particular examples of truth and beauty.

Such proponents of scholastic realism as Saint Anselm, Saint Bernard of Clairvaux, and William of Champeaux followed the tradition of Platonic idealism, which had been introduced into Christian theology by Saint Augustine.

Nominalists

According to nominalists, universals are merely the names used to describe classes of objects that share the same characteristics. Roscellinus of Compiegne was a spokesman for nominalism. Suggesting an empirical outlook, Roscellinus asserted that reality is posited in individual objects. Upon observation, certain objects are found to exhibit similar characteristics.

When carried to extremes, both realism and nominalism posed dangers for medieval Christian theology. At its logical extremity, extreme nominalism tended to the position that nothing existed that could not be apprehended through sense experience. Although the realist position was more compatible with the doctrines of the medieval Church, it too posed problems. When pushed to its logical extreme, realism could involve a total rejection of the material world. A major task of the scholastic theologians and philosophers was to reconcile the realist and nominalist positions. As we shall see later, Peter Abelard valiantly attempted to mediate the situation by advocating a stance called conceptualism.

As Haskins (1923) pointed out, we who are not philosophers take this dispute too lightly, while we consider it to simply be a matter of semantics:

> And if the differences often seem minute or unreal to our distant eye, we can make them modern enough by turning, for example, to the old question of the nature of universal conceptions, which divided the Nominalists and Realists of the Middle Ages. Are universals mere names, or have they a real existence, independent of their individual embodiments? A bit arid it all sound if we make it merely a matter of logic, but exciting enough as soon as it becomes a question of life. The essence of the Reformation lies implicit in whether we take a nominalist or a realist view of the church; the central problem of politics depends largely upon a nominalist or a realist view of the state. Upon the two sides of this last question millions of men have 'all uncouthly died,' all unconsciously too, no doubt. (p. 78)

Significance of the Medieval University

What then is our inheritance from the oldest of universities? Haskins has recounted for us several important inheritances:

1. It is, then, in institutions that the university tradition is most direct. First, the very name university, as an association of masters and scholars leading the common life of learning. Characteristic of the Middle Ages as such a corporation is, the individualistic modern world has found nothing to take its place.

2. Next, the notion of a curriculum of study, definitely laid down as regards time and subjects, tested by an examination and leading to a degree, as well as many of the degrees themselves—bachelor, as a stage

toward the mastership, master, doctor, in arts, law, medicine, and theology.

3.   Then the faculties, four or more, with their deans, and the higher officers such as chancellors and rectors, not to mention the college, wherever the residential college still survives. The essentials of university organization are clear and unmistakable, and they have been handed down in unbroken continuity for more than seven hundred years. What form of government has lasted so long?

4.   The glory of the mediaeval university was "the consecration of Learning," and the glory and the vision have not yet perished from the earth. (1923, pp. 35-36)

In addition to those cited by Haskins, Gutek shared his thoughts regarding the number of significant contributions the medieval universities made to later educational development:

1.   Modern universities bear a strong resemblance to the medieval university in organizational structure, customs, and degrees.

2.   The privileges granted to medieval scholars contributed to a respect and reverence for learning.

3.   The cosmopolitanism associated with higher education contributed to internationalize learning.

4.   Professional studies were rendered more sophisticated and specialized by the separate faculty arrangements characteristic of the medieval university.

5.   The university was a civilizing force. (1972, p. 92)

Famous Scholastic Instructors

Peter Abelard

Peter Abelard may well be the most well-known of the medieval scholars, due to a great extent because of his fateful love affair with Heloise that has been the subject of many books and plays. Born in Britanny in 1079, Peter Abelard was the son of a knight who gave up his inheritance and a military career to study philosophy.

Van Doren (1991) wrote:

> Paris had become a petri dish of theological controversy, with students flocking from one teacher to another and rioting in the streets over logical points and questions of scriptural interpretation. Abelard threw himself into these controversies, partly for the excitement of it. He also took a few private pupils, including Heloise (c. 1098-1164), the brilliant and beautiful seventeen-year-old niece of Canon Fulbert (c.960-1028) of the Cathedral of Notre Dame de Paris. (p. 115)

Abelard had been promised free housing accommodations by Canon Fulbert in exchange for tutoring his niece, Heloise. As a result of the ensuing affair, they had a son, and later they were secretly married. (Abelard was reluctant to make public the news of his marriage for fear that it would impede the development of his career.) Canon Fulbert was furious and hired several thugs to beat and castrate Abelard.

Heloise and Abelard lived apart for the remainder of their lives, but they did not desert each other. He continued to act as her spiritual advisor as she gained important ecclesiastical posts and together they published a collection of their love letters.

His most famous theological work, *Sic et Non (Yes and No)*, consisted of a collection of apparent contradictions, along with commentaries showing how contradictions might be resolved. In a fiercely, disputacious age, the book soon became very popular. Abelard also wrote a shorter work, *Scito te ipsum (Know Thyself)*, which promoted the assertion that sin is not constituted in deeds, but only in intentions. Sin is not what is done, sin is the consent of the mind to do what it knows is wrong.

Abelard is also well-known for having attempted to reconcile the two major issues facing the medieval schoolmen: nominalism versus realism; faith versus reason.

> As a synthesis of the nominalist-realist controversy Abelard offered 'conceptualism,' which held that universals had existed in the mind of God before being given form in particular objects. Universal qualities are exhibited by those classes of objects that share them; through sensation, the learner is able to recognize those discernible qualities that adhere in classes of objects. (Gutek, 1972, pp. 93-94)

In *Sic et non*, Abelard helped to formalize the scholastic educational method. He was a model teacher who exhibited the following skills:

1. His dynamic personality vitalized his lectures.

2. He was a well-prepared teacher who had carefully organized his lectures.

3. His subject matter dealt with current theological issues that were relevant to his students. (Gutek, 1972, p. 95)

Thomas Aquinas

Scholastic philosophy and education reached its zenith in the writings of Saint Thomas Aquinas (c. 1225-1274). As a member of an Italian noble family, Aquinas was enrolled at the age of five in the Benedictine Abbey of Monte Cassino. Between the ages of fourteen and eighteen, he studied liberal arts at the University of Naples, where he encountered Aristotle's philosophy through his Dominican teachers.

Against the strong objections of his parents, Aquinas decided to enter the Dominican order. The story is told that Aquinas initially escaped from the throes of his family, but his brothers were to capture him eighty miles from his home. He was bound and returned to the family castle, where he was kept prisoner for a full year as his family tried desperately to deter him from his goal (Evans, 2002).

He studied at the Monastery of the Holy Cross at Cologne from 1246 to 1252 and was ordained as a priest. In 1252, he was assigned to teach at the University of Paris, Western Europe's major theological center, where he also earned his master of theology degree and became certified as a professor of theology. From 1269 until 1272, he taught and wrote his most famous work, the *Summa theologica*.

As a student, Thomas had been ridiculed by his classmates for his size and gullibility, thus calling him the "dumb ox." According to Sproul, "The dumb ox of Aquino went on to become the supreme force of scholastic philosophy and theology" (2000, p. 66). Dahmus argued that "in Thomas scholastic thought attained its highest perfection and discovered its most eloquent exponent. Having caused the philosophical basis of Christian thought to shift from Augustinian Neo-Platonism to Aristotle provides proof of his immense influence (1995, p. 330)

As a philosopher-theologian, Aquinas was acquainted with the corpus of Christian Scripture and doctrine and Aristotelian philosophy. He spent his life seeking to integrate Christian faith and Aristotelian philosophy into a coherent worldview, and it was this pursuit that resulted in the writing of the *Summa theo-logica.*

Aquinas developed a scholastic philosophy that Gutek classified as a form of theistic realism.

1. Reality is both spiritual and material.

2. God is both ultimate Being and a personal and caring Creator.

3. Man, a rational being, can achieve knowledge of reality.

4. Man is endowed with a free will, which he exercises by making choices.

5. Objective truth and value exist as the surest guide to human conduct. (1972, p. 96)

5

Decline of Classical Education

Among those who embrace a traditionalist or classical approach to education, it would be commonly agreed that John Dewey's *Progressivism* has had an extremely detrimental effect on American education in the 20th century. In 1958, Mortimer Adler wrote:

> The traditionalists did not appear on the scene in force until almost 1930, after the reforms urged by Dewey had produced a widespread effect, first on the experimental schools and then on the considerable area of the educational system as a whole. Probably no single American's thinking has ever affected American life as rapidly and as extensively as Dewey's. (p. 148)

I agree with Adler's assertion. However, historians of education must be careful not to give too much credit or blame (depending, of course, on your perspective) to Dewey, for this approach would be far too simplistic. The philosophers and historians of education must be willing to examine and interpret the numerous events in our world's history that occurred between the Renaissance and the 20th century that affected the educational system of Europe and to a greater extent, America.

In this chapter, I will briefly share the educational philosophies of several influential educators from the Enlightenment period that paved the way for pragmatism and its sister philosophy, progressivism, to be so readily embraced.

But fortunately for humanity, even though the walls of liberal arts education that have supported classical education have been severely damaged, they still rest on a solid foundation that had endured for over 2000 years. In my concluding chapters, I will share the inspiring stories of how Mortimer Adler, Dorothy Sayers, and Douglas Wilson began to rebuild those walls, and how their efforts have been the catalyst behind a growing national movement to provide a classical education for our children.

The Enlightenment

Those involved in the age of Enlightenment, the period between the English Revolution in 1680 and the French Revolution in 1790, began the attack on classical education as expressed by the scholasticism of that era. Many of the Enlightenment thinkers criticized the philosophical assumptions of Christian theology that dominated the halls of the educational institutions. In proposing that knowledge comes from senses, experience, reason, and feelings rather than from biblical authority, and the history and tradition of Catholicism, Enlightenment thinkers or philosophes tended to undermine the traditional basis of Christian theology and education.

Holmes (2001) argued that prominent pre-Enlightenment and Enlightenment thinkers were the French philosophes Montesquieu, Voltaire, Diderot, and Rousseau; the English scholars Newton, Locke, and Hobbes; the German philosophers Kant and Lessing; the Scottish philosophers David Hume and Adam Smith; and Thomas Jefferson, Benjamin Rush, and Benjamin Franklin in the United States.

Francis Bacon

Enlightenment thinkers set their eyes on the new science that originated with the work of Francis Bacon (1561-1626). In particular, Isaac Newton (1642-1727), arguing against Descartes, held that all ideas come from sense knowledge. He contended that real knowledge was scientific knowledge, gained painstakingly through designed experiments and careful observation of natural phenomena. Newton's thought gave rise to scientific empiricism that formed the basis for a new understanding of the world. His mechanical view of nature did offer some place for God as the clockmaker of the well-ordered universe.

According to Holmes (2001), during the Elizabethan age in England, the scholastic educators had been criticized for ignoring the new science. The man who effectively led the charge in promoting the importance of science was Francis Bacon, the Lord Chancellor of England under the first Stuart king, James I. Bacon published in 1605 *The Advancement of Learning*, a critique of the educational status quo, and in 1620 *Novum Organum*, which proposed a new empirical methodology to replace the logic of Aristotle's Organon. While the religious Reformers wanted classical learning to serve the church, Bacon wanted future learning to serve society.

Bacon had studied Aristotle and Greek science as an undergraduate at Cambridge, much of which he found to be uninspiring and sterile. Bacon was disgusted that two thousand years of Aristotelianism had failed to restore humankind's dominion over God's creation. Bacon believed that God's call to Adam to subdue the earth was a mandate to advance the cause of science for the betterment of society. He was appalled that neither humanism nor scholasticism was providing new knowledge that would benefit society.

Bacon blamed the present condition on three vanities: the "contentious learning" of scholastic disputations which demonstrate only one's logical power over opponents; the "delicate learning" of humanists who toy pointlessly with beautiful words rather than with matters of substance; and the "fantastical learning" of alchemists and astrologers who seek to influence nature without knowing how it really functions. (*Advancement of Learning*, p. 198) Bacon proposed to change all three.

His desire was that higher education would no longer be just the transmitter of knowledge and values inherited from the past, but that it would also actively be involved in research and the discovery of new knowledge. This certainly seems like a noble and worthwhile goal, but these features of Baconian science, however, became the gateway to the secularization of learning. Bacon illustrated the relationship between science and Christianity with an image of two books, the book of God's works and the book of God's word. He insisted these two books be studied separately, advising his readers not to "unwisely mingle or confound these learnings (Bacon, 1937, p. 179).

Faith and learning could no longer be integrated as they had been in the medieval university. Bacon's proposal would eventually mean that religion was not relevant in "doing science." This utilitarian view made power (even if good uses of power) rather than wisdom and moral formation the goal for learning. Bacon's focus was on what one does with learning, rather than on the kind of person one became in the process.

So did Bacon succeed in uniting contemplation and action more closely than before? He connected them by making the creation mandate and the relief of human need the means by which learning should glorify God.

Bacon, of course, did not intend the wholly utilitarian approach to education that the Industrial Revolution introduced, but he did intend to combine the new science with an improved humanistic education, thereby wedding wisdom to scientific discovery.

The Enlightenment not only introduced new ideas about human nature and human society into the intellectual sphere, but also was instrumental in increasing the power of the state over education. In doing this, the control of the churches waned and weakened. Eventually what resulted were state-controlled systems of education over which churches had little or no control.

John Locke

Enlightenment thinking and practice in education, beginning with Locke and Rousseau, greatly influenced the theory and practice of education in the eighteenth century and became even more influential in the liberal and progressive approaches to education that emerged in the nineteenth and twentieth centuries. Regrettably, one finds many of these ideals incorporated in the educational philosophy of John Dewey, the foremost philosopher of education in the United States.

Locke was born on August 29, 1632, at Wrington, a small village in Somerset. He attended the prestigious Westminster School in London and later attended Christ Church College at Oxford from 1652 until 1658, where he continued his study of Greek, Hebrew, and scholastic philosophy.

In education circles, Locke is certainly well-known for his rejection of the concept of innate ideas advocated by Descartes. Locke argued that all ideas come from reflection on experience. Locke applied his ideas to education in his highly influential *Some Thoughts on Education*, published in 1693. His book was the result of a series of letters of advice Locke had written to his friend Edward Clarke regarding the process of home schooling children. Viewing the child as a tabula rasa (a blank slate), Locke assigned critical importance to early educational processes. For him, education was mainly a moral affair since its aim was to produce good persons. With regard to moral education, he opposed the doctrine of original sin and argued that virtue could be taught by purely secular means. In his view, children were to be reasoned with from the earliest years.

> It will perhaps be wondered that I mention reasoning with children: and yet I cannot but think that the true way of dealing with them. They understand it as early as they do language; and, if I misobserve not, they love to be treated as rational creatures sooner than is imagined. 'Tis a pride should be cherished in them and, as much as can be, made the great instrument to turn them by. (*Some Thoughts Concerning Education*, section 81)

Intellectually, Locke stressed the importance of literacy, history, and science, but he was not an advocate of classical education's emphasis on the importance of studying Latin.

Latin I look upon as absolutely necessary to a gentleman; and indeed, custom, which prevails over everything, has made it so much a part of education that even those children are whipped to it and made to spend many hours of their precious time uneasily in Latin who, after they are once gone from school, are never to have more to do with it as long as they live. Can there be anything more ridiculous than that a father should waste his own money and his son's time in setting him to learn the Roman language, when at the same time he designs him for a trade? (*Some Thought Concerning Education*, 164)

Jean-Jacques Rousseau

According to Elias (2002), the most famous Enlightenment writer on education was Jean-Jacques Rousseau (1712-1778). In 1792, he published *Emile*, a book that greatly angered Christian and especially Catholic educators of the time. "Yet no book in the history of education, with the possible exception of Plato's *Republic*, has had more influence in educational theorizing and practice" (p. 135).

The Archbishop of Paris condemned *Emile*, causing Rousseau to flee to England. The strong reaction against *Emile* was caused by Rousseau's extreme attack on Catholic education. Through its domination of the schools, Rousseau accused the Catholic Church of sabotaging the quest for truth. (I for one have a difficult time accepting that the "father of modern education" gave away all five of his illegitimate children. In his quest for truth, I would be curious to know how he justified such behavior.) In *Emile*, a romantic and utopian work, Rousseau charged the traditional views on child rearing and education with excessive constraints. He proposed that children be allowed to develop according to their natural proclivities. Rousseau was dead set against treating children as if they were small adults. His challenge to educators and parents was to do exactly the opposite of what was usually done regarding the discipline of their children. Rousseau rejected such supernatural doctrines as original sin, asserting that individuals were born good but corrupted by society. The famous opening sentence of *Emile* reads: "God makes all things good; man meddles with them and they become evil. He forces one soil to yield the products of another, one tree to bear another's fruit" (Rousseau, 1961, p. 5).

Rousseau believed that students should be allowed to use their gifts of sensation, memory, and understanding in their quest for learning, which came naturally through play and observation. The role of the teacher was not to direct or instruct but to aid children to learn from experience. For moral education of children, he advised that children should learn from social experiences rather than from religion.

Rousseau's theory of education expounded in *Emile* received additional attention in his later work *Social Contract*. In the latter, he proposed a utopian vision of the ideal society in which education played an important social role.

Emmanuel Kant

In his book *On Education,* Emmanuel Kant (1724-1804) attempted to elaborate on many of Rousseau's ideas on education with a stronger philosophical foundation in German idealism. Kant tried to strike a balance between teaching children to be submissive to those in authority and children's necessary exercising of free will. This balance was to be achieved by granting higher levels of freedom when students had demonstrated higher levels of discipline. However, this freedom was not allowed to interfere with the freedom of others (Elias, 2002). Also, as a deist, Kant placed little emphasis on the importance of studying the Bible or the church's catechism.

Johann Pestalozzi

The Swiss educator Johann Pestalozzi (1746-1827) is well known for his attempt to implement the Enlightenment ideas of Rousseau and Kant into actual practice by establishing experimental schools for poor children. According to Elias, "Pestalozzi began with the principle that human nature is inherently good and contains the potential for intellectual and moral development that can best be achieved through the exercise of love and kindness by parents and teachers" (2002, p. 142).

Frederick Froebel

A further systematization of these Enlightenment ideas came from Frederick Froebel's (1782-1852) effort to develop an organic approach to education in his *The Education of Man* (1826). Froebel drew from the writings of Rousseau but also from his own teaching experiences. Froebel stressed the importance of beginning formal education at the early age of three. The German term for his school was *kleinkinderbeschaftingungsanstalt,* which in America simply became known as kindergarten.

For Froebel, early childhood education was to focus around activities such as play, music, and physical activity. Froebel can be credited for creating a new level of respect for children and their individuality.

Elias (2002) argued that the greatest stumbling block for most educators has been the Enlightenment's somewhat naive view of the human person. While Enlightenists viewed the child as naturally good, the traditionalists reviewed the child as being affected by the result of original sin and thus being inclined to do wrong. Thus, the teaching of the Bible and the catechism to young children was a necessity.

As we have seen, the Enlightenment theories of education tended to minimize the role of religion in education, especially in the education of the young. These criticisms continue to be cited to this day by those who oppose the twentieth-century progressive education, which drew in part on the educational ideas and experiments of Enlightenment educators.

William James and Pragmatism

Background

William James was a New Yorker, born in the Astor Hotel in 1842. William James's grandfather, "William James of Albany," had arrived with other Scotch-Irish immigrants in 1789 and in Albany he earned a fortune large enough to make his descendants comfortable. William's father, Henry Senior, tried Princeton Theological Seminary, but he could not accept the strict Calvinists who saw the world and their lives foreordained by a very autocratic deity.

In the late 1850s, the family traveled to Europe for several years where Henry Senior tried to secure a cosmopolitan education in faith and learning for his children. In 1861, as the Civil War broke out, James left home to begin his studies at Harvard. The year the war ended he spent in Brazil with scientist Louis Agassiz, learning to observe the natural world with great care. For the next four years, James studied medicine. He graduated from Harvard in 1870 with a medical degree, but he was not interested in practicing medicine. Two years later, he was offered a job as an assistant professor at Harvard, where he remained for the next thirty-five years.

His numerous books on philosophy and religion include:

1. *The Principles of Psychology* (1890)

2. *The Will to Believe* (1897)

3. *Varieties of Religious Experience* (1902)

4. *Pragmatism* (1907)

5. *A Pluralistic Universe* (1909)

6. *The Meaning of Truth* (1909)

7. *Some Problems of Philosophy* (posthumously, 1911)

8. *Essays in Radical Empiricism* (posthumously, 1912)

Introduction to Pragmatism

While most of the philosophical movements that affect our society originated in Europe, pragmatism is homegrown. In layman's terms, it is a philosophy that emphasizes what is practical and expedient. If pragmatism had a motto, it would be, "Where there's a will, there's a way."

Historically, pragmatism developed as a category of the broad philosophical perspective of secularism. Its birth follows the period of the Enlightenment in the seventeenth and eighteenth centuries in which philosophers glorified reason and the scientific method. Ultimately, its origin could be traced back to Heraclitus.

According to Kneller:

> Pragmatism has been known by several names—"pragmaticism" as coined by Charles Peirce, "functionalism," "instrumentalism," and "experimentalism." In his later years, Dewey preferred experimentalism to instrumentalism, partly be cause the latter sounded too materialistic. The principal themes of pragmatism are (1) the reality of change, (2) the essentially social and biological nature of man, (3) the relativity of values, and (4) the use of critical intelligence. (1971, p. 13)

James first employed the term pragmatism in a lecture entitled "Philosophical Conceptions and Practical Results," delivered before the Philosophical Union at the University of California at Berkeley in August 1898. He was borrowing the term from his friend and sometime colleague Charles Sanders Peirce, who had first developed it in an essay that appeared in *Popular Science Monthly* in 1878 entitled "How to Make Our Ideas Clear."

Durant (1926) wrote that James believed that the cosmos is not a closed and harmonious system, but a battleground of cross-currents and conflicting purposes. Thus, the term universe is a misstatement according to James. The cosmos is not a uni-verse but a multi-verse, consisting of cross-currents and warring forces that help decide issues. Nothing is irrevocably settled and all action matters. James believed that it was useless to accept that the chaos of this world is the result of one consistent will.

Pragmatic Truth

In Lecture 6 from *Pragmatism: A New Name for Some Old Ways of Thinking* (1907), James wrote:

> Truth, as any dictionary will tell you, is a property of certain ideas. It means their 'agreement,' as falsity means their disagreement, with 'reality.' Pragmatists and intellectualists both accept this definition as a matter of course. They begin to quarrel only after the question is raised as to what may precisely be meant by the term 'agreement,' and what by the term 'reality,' when reality is taken as something for our ideas to agree with. (pp. 76-77)

He went on to say:

> Pragmatism, on the other hand, asks its usual question. "Grant an idea or belief to be true," it says, "what concrete difference will its being true make in anyone's actual life? How will the truth be realized? What experiences will be different from those which it would obtain if the belief were false?
>
> What, in short, is the truth's cash-value in experiential terms?" The moment pragmatism asks this question, it sees the answer: *True ideas are those that we can assimilate, validate, corroborate, and verify. False ideas are those that we cannot.* That is the practical difference it makes to us to have true ideas; that, therefore, is the meaning of truth, for it is all that truth is known as. The truth of an idea is not a stagnant property inherent in it. Truth *happens* to an idea. It *becomes* true, is *made* true by events. Its verity is in fact an event, a process: the process namely of its verifying itself, its veri*fication*. Its validity is the process of its valid*ation*. (p. 77)

Thus, according to James, truth is a process, and pragmatism therefore examines the results of an idea to determine its truthfulness. Truth is not determined by Aristotle's "prime mover" or the God of Judeo-Christian beliefs. Truth never looks back, only forward to determine veracity.

Metaphysics

Sproul (1986) in his analysis of James's religious beliefs wrote:

> One of the great ironies of American history occurred at Harvard University in the nineteenth century. Students of philosophy who specialized in concerns of a metaphysical nature formed the Metaphysics Club. Three classmates who were members of that club—William James, Charles Peirce, and Oliver Wendell Holmes became, along with John Dewey, the leading spokesmen in

America for the philosophy of pragmatism. The irony is that, historically, pragmatism grew out of this group at Harvard who were committed to the precepts of metaphysics. The Metaphysics Club produced a violent and anti-metaphysical philosophy. (p. 82)

How would James respond to the oldest problem in philosophy—the existence and nature of God? He believed that there was no need of going beyond the experience process to a soul, because the soul is merely the sum of our mental life. However, James was convinced of the reality of some type of spiritual world:

I firmly disbelieve, myself, that our human experience is the highest form of experience extant in the universe. I believe rather that we stand in much the same relation to the whole of the universe as our canine and feline pets do to the whole of human life. They inhabit our drawing rooms and libraries. They take part in scenes of whose significance they have no inkling. They are merely tangent to curves of history, the beginnings and ends and forms of which pass wholly beyond their ken. So we are tangent to the wider life of things. (Pragmatism, 1907, p. 318)

Sproul (1986) raised the question of how William James would approach religion. Sproul answered his question with this example:

Suppose you were a Christian and you went to Dr. James to describe your faith. You would go to his study and he would say, 'All right, tell me about your Christian experience.' You would tell him that you grew up in such and such a home, and that you had a crisis experience when you were twenty-one and were converted to Christianity. He would begin to probe to see how your attitudes changed, how your behavior changed, how your inner feelings changed. He would ask, 'Has this been a positive experience for you or a negative one?' You would answer, 'It has been a positive experience for *me*.'

So James would respond, 'For you, religion works. It helps you cope. It helps you make it in this world. So for *you*, religion is *good* and religion is *true*.' (p. 83)

Pragmatism and Education

According to Kneller (1971), James believed, that since man is the measure of all things, students should be allowed to determine their own reality regarding what would be important for them to study. Students' interests should not be undermined but allowed to grow as part of the process of determining truth. Dewey did not concur wholeheartedly with this premise, arguing that experts should be actively involved in determining subject matter.

Kneller also stated:

> The pragmatist maintains that since reality is created by a person's interaction with his environment, the child must study the world as it affects him. Just as the child cannot be considered apart from the environment in which he lives, so the school cannot be separated from life itself. Education *is* life and not a preparation for it. Formal subject matter should be linked wherever possible to the immediate problems that the child faces and that society is concerned to solve. (1971, p. 14)

After the death of James, a paper was found on his desk on which he had written his sad and discouraging final sentences: "There is no conclusion. What has concluded that we might conclude in regard to it? There are no fortunes to be told and there is no advice to be given. Farewell" (cited in Kneller, 1971, p. 15).

John Dewey and Educational Progressivism

It is commonly agreed that John Dewey was the major spokesperson for the school of thought known as progressivism, although initially Dewey preferred to call it "instrumentalism" because knowledge was the "instrument" that guided the reactions between humans and their environment. His most well known book related to education was undoubtedly *Democracy and Education* published in 1916.

Dewey was born in 1859 in Burlington, Vermont, and died at the age of ninety-two in 1952. He attended public schools and the University of Vermont. Upon graduation, he taught high school for two years, but decided to pursue a career in philosophy as a graduate student at John Hopkins University. He obtained his doctorate in 1884 and spent nine of the next ten years teaching at the University of Michigan. In 1894, he moved to the recently founded University of Chicago where he founded and directed a laboratory school. In 1904, he was invited to join the department of philosophy at Columbia University where he remained until his retirement from active teaching in 1930.

In the following section, I highlight briefly the major components of a "progressive education." Hearing the term, we naturally tend to think of "progress." However, I would contend progressive education had an extremely detrimental effect on American schools during the past century.

Purpose and Role of the School

The school is viewed as an involved and ongoing institution of society that contributes to the supporting community. A good school reflects the norms of society and seeks greater human happiness for its students. Schools should prepare the youth for leadership and above all the responsibilities for democratic participation in our society (Howick, 1971).

Curriculum and Method

The content should be like life, never compartmentalized, but overlapping. The classroom should be a miniature of the good life outside and should resemble real living. Planning of activities should be a joint exercise between the teacher and students. Methodology consists of group learning, audio-visual aides, field trips, and project-units (Howick, 1971).

Role of the Teacher

Howick (1971) shared that according to progressivism, the teacher's task is to provide an environment that facilitates the students' activities. As a facilitator, his or her role is to never be obtrusive, always be democratic, and respect the natural rights of all. Providing motivation for learning is more important than dispensing of information.

Thus, the child is the center of the educational experience, not the teacher. The students must have the freedom to discover "truth" and to develop knowledge by themselves. Truth, according to pragmatism, can be "made" by the students by observing consequences of actions. If something works, it is true.

Diane Ravitch, former Assistant Secretary of Education, is a prolific writer, having published numerous books dealing with the history of education in America. Her recent book, *Left Back* (2000), focused on the numerous educational reforms of the past century.

In 1983, she published *The Troubled Crusade*, a book that dealt with the advent of "progressivism" and its impact on our educational system. Ravitch wrote that by the 1940s, progressive education had become the dominant American pedagogy. It even came to be commonly referred to as "modern education," the "new education," or the "good education." Prospective teachers in our universities were being taught that the old-fashioned education was rigid, subject-centered, and authoritarian while modern education was flexible, child-centered, democratic, and progressive.

Progressive educators rejected the belief that schools existed to improve intellectual functioning through the use of books and the traditional subjects such as history, English, science, and math. They called for schools that used experiences and projects instead of reading assignments, which was too passive. Activities needed to be jointly planned by the teachers and students, with an emphasis on cooperation instead of competitiveness as exemplified by giving of grades.

Our high schools changed dramatically during this time. From 1900 until 1950, our high school enrollment went from half a million students to over five million. In 1900, the curriculum was strongly academic. However, by 1950 the curriculum had been diluted by numerous vocational and nonacademic courses. Here we have the advent of the "shopping mall curriculum." With retention of students as a strong driving force, high schools began to add these various courses. Like shopping in a mall, there was something for everyone. Thus, the new comprehensive high school began to take on numerous societal and parent responsibilities.

The catalyst behind this new purpose for high schools can be traced to a major educational report in 1918 known as the *Cardinal Principles of Secondary Education.* High schools existed to meet the following needs of the students:

1. Health

2. Command of fundamental processes

3. Worthy home-membership

4. Vocation

5. Citizenship

6. Worthy use of leisure

7. Ethical character

Contrasted to this is the "Committee of Ten" report of 1893, which recommended that all high school students should receive a liberal arts education through the study of English, foreign languages, mathematics, history, and science.

Even John Dewey himself in 1938, writing in *Experience and Education,* rebuked the extremists who had corrupted education by actively trying to remove traditional subject matter from our schools.

As an aid in evaluating your own philosophy of education, I invite you to analyze Table 2 at the end of this book. Chall, in her book *The Academic Achieve-*

ment Challenge: What Really Works in the Classroom?, shared this chart to illuminate the differences between progressive and classical instruction. She explained in her book that she referred to progressive education as student-centered instruction and classical education as teacher-centered. She also reminded her readers that reality would not necessarily dictate an either-or approach in using these criteria.

6

The Resurgence of Classical Education

LIFE OF DOROTHY L. SAYERS
AND "THE LOST TOOLS OF LEARNING"

In 1947, Dorothy L. Sayers, well-known for the "Lord Peter Wimsey" mysteries and later in her career for a translation of Dante's *Divine Comedy*, made a speech at a Vacation Class at Oxford that was to become a major catalyst for the resurgence of classical education in America. Her now well-known address is indirectly responsible for launching hundreds of classical schools, most of which operate from a distinctly Christian perspective (Wilson, 1991).

In her famous address, which she entitled "The Lost Tools of Learning," she lamented the fact that Western schools are no longer effectively utilizing the great and necessary tools of learning: grammar, dialectic, and rhetoric. What are these all-important tools? Allow me to postpone answering the quintessential question and begin by sharing facets of Sayers' life. As a translator of Dante's *Divine Comedy*, she was concerned that the scholarly world criticized her as a mystery writer who was dabbling outside her realm. My contention is that she was extremely well-educated and her background epitomizes the type of education we should seek for our children and ourselves.

Brief Biography of Dorothy Sayers's Life

The following summation of Dorothy Sayer's life and her impact on classical education is paraphrased from Dale Alzina's biography entitled *Maker and Craftsman: The Story of Dorothy L. Sayers* published in 1978.

Early Life

Dorothy Leigh Sayers was born at Oxford on June 13, 1893. She was the only child of the Reverend Henry Sayers and his wife, Helen Mary. Her father was headmaster of the University Cathedral Choir School. After graduating from Oxford in 1879, he had been ordained a minister in the Church of England. Mr. Sayers was not only a good musician, but he was also a classics scholar who taught Latin in his school.

In describing her own childhood, Dorothy told about the kind of child she had been:

> "Looking back on myself, since I am the child I know best and the only child I can pretend to know from inside, I recognize three stages of development. These, in a rough' and-ready fashion, I will call the Poll-Parrot, the Pert, and, the Poetic." (*Lost Tools of Learning,* 1948, pp. 14-15)

From about nine years to eleven, she was the poll-parrot, who liked to memorize lists and gibberish like advertising jingles. From twelve to fourteen she was pert, fond of contradicting her elders. In the poetic period from fifteen on, she was a moody and preoccupied adolescent.

When Dorothy was growing up, most middle-class fathers did not educate their daughters in the same manner as their sons. Girls usually stayed at home and were taught languages like French or German, drawing, music, and social manners—first by their mothers or nurses and then by the governess. Rev. Sayers realized very early that Dorothy was extremely bright and planned for her to have a university education. He began the preparation by teaching her Latin.

Their Latin lesson became a daily event. Once Dorothy knew enough Latin, she and her father marched with Caesar's army, built Roman walls with Balbo, and admired the conduct of Cornelia, the Roman matron who brought up her children to be good citizens. Although her father was not an exciting teacher, those early years were fun, and at that time she liked Latin better than French, which she was also beginning to learn.

She grew up in a house where books were all about. The enormous numbers of books that Dorothy considered her special friends appear all through her own writings, and many of her characters quote from them. They range from Mother Goose to the poems of T. S. Eliot. As a girl she especially adored romantic adventure stories like *The Scarlet Pimpernel* or *The Three Musketeers* or *The Prisoner of Zenda,* while she also read the detective stories of Conan Doyle and Wilkie Collins and the stories of Edgar Wallace.

In 1905, when Dorothy was almost thirteen, her father hired a special French governess to teach her German and French. By the time she was fifteen, Dorothy was fluent in both French and German, but she no longer liked Latin because, instead of being able to read novels and poems and plays, she had to work her way line by line through boring Latin classics like Cicero's speeches to the Roman Senate.

In January 1909, Dorothy, who was almost sixteen, was sent away to The Godolphin School, a boarding school in the old cathedral town of Salisbury. Not many Godolphin students cared about having careers, but Dorothy had been sent to Godolphin primarily to be sure she would later be accepted by Oxford University. Although she did not enjoy her experiences at Godolphin School and was not very popular, she did begin to apply herself and took her studies very seriously. In 1909, she took the standardized examinations that determined the next level of schooling and what level of scholarship if any. In the areas of "Written French" and "Spoken French and German," she had done better than any other candidate in England who had taken both language examinations.

Later Dorothy went to Oxford to take the formal entrance examinations. When the results of the test came out, she had won one of the best scholarships available at the time. It was called the Gilchrist Scholarship, and its winner went to Somerville College, which was considered the toughest women's college academically.

Life at Oxford

When Dorothy arrived by train at the beginning of the Michaelmas, or fall term in 1912, the women's colleges were still not officially part of the university, and the women students were not granted university degrees. This is why it is often said that Dorothy was one of the first women to get an Oxford degree. However, there had been women students at Oxford for two generations before her, and she did not really think of herself as a pioneer.

In a college full of students who liked to have endless discussions on politics, religion and art, Dorothy was soon known as one of the most eager and argumentative debaters. She and her friends later suspected that these midnight sessions had been the most valuable part of their college life.

The university granted degrees, based on its examinations, even though no student actually attended Oxford University as such. All students were either Scholars, Exhibitioners, or Commoners, and the male students in each group wore different kinds of academic gowns. Scholars were the brightest students, like Dorothy, who had won the biggest awards. Exhibitioners, like J. R. R. Tolkien, had not done quite so well; the Commoners were simply students who paid their own way. In 1915, Sayers completed her academic requirements, but as a woman, she was not yet eligible to receive a degree.

For her first job, Dorothy chose to do what most Oxford women graduates did: she got a job teaching in a girls' school. Her first job was as the Modern Languages teacher at Hull High School for Girls. Meanwhile, in 1916 when she was twenty-three, Dorothy had a real triumph. Her first volume of poetry, called *Op I* (or *First Work* in English), was published in Oxford by Basil Blackwell. Ironically however, by 1917 Dorothy had become convinced that teaching was a mistake for her professionally because it was too demanding. Basil Blackwell, her publisher, hired her to work for his company.

In 1919, women's education moved forward with the passage of what was called the "Women's Statute." Women could now be granted university degrees and become full members of the university community. For the first time too, women at Oxford were required to wear academic dress. On the 14th of October in 1920, a warm, sunny day, a large crowd gathered at Sheldonian Theatre to watch the first women—that included Dorothy L. Sayers—granted university degrees.

In 1922, after another short spell teaching high school, Dorothy got a job as an advertising copywriter. While she was learning to live in London, Dorothy became a published novelist for the first time. *Whose Body?*, her first Lord Peter mystery, came out in 1923, when she was thirty. From the beginning, Sayers's writings were about the Christian world, in which man is a fallen creature but able to choose between good and evil in a place where such choices matter. *Whose Body?* was not a best-seller, but it did well enough for her publisher to agree to publish Dorothy's second Lord Peter mystery, *Clouds of Witness*.

Private Life

Biographical sketches published during her lifetime mentioned that she and her husband had an adopted son whose name was John Anthony Fleming. At her death, her public learned a little more about him because he was her sole heir. Dorothy and her husband had unofficially adopted Anthony when he was about ten, at the time he was sent to boarding school. At her death, he was a thirty-four-year-old economist, recently married, and living in London. However, it was not until 1975 that it was disclosed in a book about Dorothy by Janet Hitchman that John Anthony Fleming was Dorothy's own son, born out of wedlock in 1924, when she was thirty. Two years after Anthony's birth, in 1926, when she was thirty-four, Dorothy married Oswald Arthur Fleming, a divorced man who was twelve years older than she.

While Dorothy had been pursuing a successful writing career, Great Britain was living through a series of troubles. During the 1930s, the Great Depression had put millions of people out of work. The old king George V had died, and the Prince of Wales, now Edward VIII, had reigned only a few months before abdicating because the Church of England would not allow him to marry a divorced woman. Now Great Britain was entrenched in the Second World War.

Dorothy developed her own position regarding the war. Having gotten into this grim situation, England had a responsibility to free the world from an intolerable evil. With her understanding of history and Christian doctrine, she believed individuals do have the chance to choose how they will act in every situation, even though heaven on earth will never be realized.

The Sunday after war had been declared, the Sunday Times printed one of her guest editorials, entitled "What Do We Believe?" In it, she remarked that a faith is not meant to be a comfort to us in bad times, but a truth about ourselves.

In 1941, when she was close to fifty, Dorothy began work on a new kind of project. A series of books called *Bridgeheads* by various authors was planned to help the country cope with the unpleasant realities of wartime. Dorothy's book was called *The Mind of the Maker,* a commentary, based upon her own experience with the statements made in the Christian creeds.

In her book, she used many examples from her own writing, but basic to her whole discussion is her understanding of God as a maker or artist. The characteristic common to God and man is the desire and ability to make things. To Dorothy, we are most alive when we are using that power, each in his or her own way.

Translator of Dante

During an air raid in World War II, after her husband yelled at her to hurry up, she rushed downstairs from her study clutching the first volume of her grandmother Sayers' Temple edition of Dante's *Divine Comedy.* The book had the medieval Italian text of the poem on one page and a prose English translation across from it on the opposite page. Dorothy did not know modern Italian, but with the help of her French and what Latin she could remember, she managed to read the first part, *Inferno,* fairly well. By the time the "all clear" finally sounded, she was absolutely fascinated by Dante, whom she had never taken the time to read. Reading Dante for the first time at the age of fifty-one, she found his *Divine Comedy* the most exciting adventure story she had read since her childhood.

Early in 1945, she wrote to Penguin Books and proposed that she translate Dante's *Divine Comedy* into modern English verse. Amazingly, by this time she had already taught herself how to read medieval Italian. The result was that she devoted a significant portion of the rest of her professional life to winning an audience for another artist's work.

Penguin Books accepted her offer to begin translating the *Inferno*, while at the same time she dismayed her fans by announcing that she would write no more about her famous mystery sleuth, Lord Peter Wimsey.

In the spring of 1950, when he was sixty-eight, her husband Mac died. Dorothy found his death all the more depressing because at the time she was working so hard on her Dante. It was during 1950 that the University of Durham made Dorothy an honorary Doctor of Literature. She bought herself a new fur coat to celebrate, and it was said in Witham she never took it off again. She was always pleased when people called her, quite correctly, "Dr. Sayers."

She continued to give many talks, often on Dante, and to work on her translation of his *Purgatory*, the place where the souls of sinners are re-educated so they are ready to meet God. She felt that *Purgatory*, while the least known, is the most tender and human part of the *Comedy*, giving the reader the appalling fascination of hell or the intellectual severity of heaven. Dorothy's translation of *Purgatory* came out in 1955 and she began working on *Paradise*.

Dorothy started her final day, Tuesday, December 17, 1957, by taking a train to London to finish her Christmas shopping. A friend who saw her that day would later comment that she looked very tired. Later that evening, Dorothy took the train back to Witham, where she caught a taxi to take her home.

Like a mystery novel, what happened after she returned home remains unknown. On Wednesday morning, her gardener-handyman discovered lights on in her bedroom and her treasured fur coat and bag dumped on the bed. He found Dorothy, dead, at the foot of the stairs. Her postmortem declared that she had died of heart failure. She was sixty-four years old.

"The Lost Tools" of Learning: What Are They and Why Are They So Important?

For a complete copy of Sayer's essay, please refer to the appendix. Sayers lamented in her essay that we have succeeded in teaching our students subjects, but we have failed overall in teaching them how to think. In order to correct this, we must turn back the hands of time four or five hundred years to the point in our history that medieval schools employed the tools of the trivium—*grammar, logic, and rhetoric.*

Before we look at these tools, let me briefly explain why they were so important. In the medieval universities, students were trained in the art of the quadrivium, which consisted of the study of mathematics, music, astronomy, and geometry. The study of science included the natural sciences along with the moral sciences such as the study of history, politics, law, and theology. Upon completion of the quadrivium, the student was allowed to specialize in the areas of law, medicine, or theology. Students entering the university were expected to have mastered the arts of the trivium. Thus, they would have the necessary tools for learning. Unfortunately, so many students entering our universities today lack these basic and necessary skills of the trivium. It is no wonder that our university leaders bemoan how they must spend so much of their resources on teaching basic skills to their entering freshmen.

Grammar Stage

The following sections provide my brief summations of the concepts she referred to in her essay. During the early years (kindergarten through 5th or 6th grades), students study the Grammar portion of the trivium. During this stage that Sayers called the Poll-Parrot, learning by heart is easy and enjoyable. However, reasoning is quite difficult. Each specific subject has its own grammar (basic skills for study and pertinent facts). We are familiar with English grammar but often fail to realize that each subject has its own grammar as well. Students memorize multiplication tables, learn geography skills and facts, memorize important dates, and learn plant and animal classifications; anything that lends itself to easy repetition and assimilation by the mind. Teachers often create chants or songs that facilitate the memorization of such information.

English

Verse and prose should be memorized and students should be exposed to classical myths and European legends. The famous stories should be enjoyed and not overly used in teaching the techniques of grammar. In order to lay the groundwork for the Rhetoric, students should be actively involved in recitation, individually or as a group.

History

Sayers called for the grammar of history to consist of dates, events, anecdotes, and personalities. Students must have a "peg" on which later historical knowledge can be hung. Using timelines is essential. The mere mention of a given date should call up a strong visual picture containing multiple facets of the specific time period.

As is not the case in most American schools, history serves as the cornerstone for learning in many Christian and Classical schools that belong to the ACCS. Students actively study ancient and modern world history beginning in first grade. In the ACCS schools, as well as other types of Christian schools, history is viewed as the manifestation of God's divine plan. Augustine thought that God was involved in all of human affairs and that society would continue to move in the direction of righteousness and peace.

In our American schools, we have done our students an injustice by beginning the teaching of history in 5th grade with the discovery of the new world. Our students not only fail to realize the historical setting for this great adventure, but they also falsely believe that the United States is the focal point of all history.

Geography

Geography should be taught in a factual manner that includes using maps and visual presentations of customs, costumes, flora, and so on. Sayers also added that it certainly could not hurt to have students memorize facts such as capitals, mountains, and rivers. As a former 5th grade teacher, I know students take great pride in memorizing such trivia.

Science

Students enjoy classifying entities and knowing the names and properties of things. Knowing that a whale is not a fish or a bat is not a bird is exciting to young students.

Mathematics

Students must learn their arithmetic tables. For example, learning of the multiplication facts at a young age is much more enjoyable and less taxing than it is for older students. Sayers would be even further disillusioned with certain educators of today who advocate doing away with such memorization because we have calculators.

Theology

Although Sayers recognized that not all would agree with her promotion of studying theology, she contended that those students who do not possess this knowledge would have an education full of loose ends. Theology is the mistress-science that must include at this age a study of the Old and New Testaments presented as parts of the narrative of Creation, Rebellion, and Redemption. The Creeds, the Lord's Prayer, and the Ten Commandments should also be studied.

Latin

This period also includes the study of a foreign language, of which Sayers strongly recommends the study of Latin.

Logic, or Dialectic Stage

In about the seventh grade, the student enters the logic/dialectic stage or as Dorothy Sayers called it—the pert stage. The students are no longer interested in just learning facts; now they want more. They want to analyze subjects in a deeper fashion: what, who, where, how, why of a subject. For example, they are no longer content to just know about World War II. They want to understand the events that led up to our involvement. Previously students would have memorized December 7, 1941, as the day Pearl Harbor was bombed. Now they want to know why this event took place.

In the grammar stage, observation and memorization are critical; in the dialectic stage discursive, or logical reasoning is highly important. As Latin grammar plays a key role in the grammar stage, the study of formal logic is critical to the dialectic. She bemoaned the modern approach of basing decisions on our intuitiveness and less on reasoning. The knowledge of syllogisms does not provide the answers for all problems but it does help train the young mind to detect and expose invalid inferences.

Language

Students must work on increasing their vocabulary levels and concentrating on syntax and analysis. Students should also study the historical development of our language.

Reading

Students must move on to essays, argument, and criticism, and they should try to imitate these styles of writing. Many lessons should incorporate the use of debates and dramatic performances should be added to the rhetorical practices.

Mathematics

Algebra, geometry, and advanced types of arithmetic are added during this stage. Math should be viewed as a sub-department of logic.

History

In addition to continuing the study of content, students greatly enjoy ethical discussions regarding the actions of leaders from the past or even the present. Students must be able to recognize both sides of controversies.

Theology

Biblical topics provide material for argument regarding conduct and morals just as geography and science also provide arenas for discussion. Sayers could never have envisioned that students in the relatively near future would be discussing the morality of such scientific topics as cloning.

Life Experiences

Sayers pointed out that the newspapers are full of examples of fallacious reasoning and muddleheaded arguments that provide good examples for discussion. An umpire's decision is even food for thought if treated in a proper manner. Having been a sports' official for many years, this example strikes close to home.

Rhetoric Stage

During the Rhetoric Stage, or as Dorothy Sayers would say, the Poetic Stage, the goal is to adorn "truth" with beauty. The working definition of rhetoric is that students must learn to express themselves well in a persuasive, aesthetically pleasing form. As they continue to acquire content and dialectic skills, persuasive writing, speech, debate, and drama are actively stressed.

During this stage, students should recognize that although they have studied "subjects" all knowledge is one. To accomplish this, the mistress-science of theology should be employed. Also during this stage, the study of Latin may be dropped for those who prefer the study of a modern language. She also acknowledged that all students would not be able to compete at the same level in mathematics. Therefore, advanced levels of mathematics should not be required of all students. As the modern-day educator, Theodore Sizer of the "Coalition of Essential Schools," so strongly promoted in his book *Horace's Compromise* (1984), Sayers called for a culminating project—the presentation and public defense of a thesis.

As an additional note on her essay, allow me to remind us that the first segment of her essay informed us of the sorry state of affairs regarding our educational system. What we must never lose sight of is that her assertions were made in 1947. Many times I have spoken to parents who express their desire for their children to have a strong classical education, such as they wrongly believe they received in the fifties, sixties, and seventies. Those of us who are baby boomers only disillusion ourselves by longing for the education of recent decades. As Dorothy L. Sayers vehemently contends, we must be willing to travel back several hundred years to re-discover the tools that were then in place.

Doug Wilson and Recovering the Lost Tools of Learning

In 1947 Sayers' essay was published in the *Hibbert Journal* and in 1948 it was published in a booklet form by E.T. Heron & Company. The essay first traveled to America when it was published in William Buckley's *National Review* in 1959. Twenty years later the magazine would again publish it. Buckley quotes from Sayers in his book *Up from Liberalism* published in 1959:

> I shall not here be contending what Miss Sayers, whose dismay is shared by many observers of American education, contends, namely that the faculty for logical thought is a skill of which the entire contemporary generation has been bereft. (p. 37)

Thankfully, Douglas Wilson, a pastor in Moscow, Idaho, also shared Sayers' concern for the state of our educational system. Through recent correspondence, Mr. Wilson shared with me that he had first read Sayer's essay as it appeared in *National Review*, while he was in the navy. When he began to consider starting his own Christian school, he went to his local library to retrieve another copy.

With a daughter approaching kindergarten, he resolved that she would be in the first class of a new school that would seek to embrace the principles that Sayers' essay endorsed. In 1980, the Logos School opened its doors to 19 students, operating out of a church basement. Today, it has almost 300 students and has produced numerous high school graduates.

Thanks to Wilson's insight and dedication to seeking the best education for his daughter, an educational movement was born. In 1991, he published a book entitled: *Recovering the Lost Tools of Learning: An Approach to Distinctively Christian Education*. The book helped drive the formation of a number of schools based on the Logos model. In 1993, Logos School hosted a conference to explain the principles of classical education to the many interested parties. As a result of this conference, a new entity was birthed—the Association of Classical and Christian Schools (ACCS).

The Association began with seven charter schools in 1994—The Christian Leadership Academy in Michigan, The Geneva School in Florida, Logos School in Idaho, Providence Academy in Wisconsin, Providence Classical Christian School in Washington, Regents School of Austin in Texas, and Whitefield School in Georgia. Today the ACCS has over 110 member schools in 39 states and 5 countries. In addition there are over 25 home school associations that are affiliate members.

MORTIMER ADLER AND THE PAIDEIA PROPOSAL

Adler's Background

Mortimer Adler was born in 1902. During his career, he authored and co-authored more than thirty books, ranging from religious to scientific studies (Rich, 1992). His educational background is unusual. At the age of fourteen, he dropped out of De Witt Clinton High School in New York City. As editor of the school newspaper, he refused to comply with the principal's request to suspend a fellow student from the staff whose grades had fallen below par. Adler later lied to the principal concerning this matter and was suspended from all extracurricular activities. He persuaded his parents to let him drop out of school and go to work (Adler, 1977).

Adler soon secured a job as a copyboy for the New York *Sun*. Within a month, he was promoted to secretary to the editor in chief for which he received a salary of five dollars per week, and on occasion even authored editorials for the newspaper. While working for the *Sun* he started attending night classes through the

Extension Division of Columbia University to improve his skills as a writer. In 1920, he quit the *Sun* to begin studying for the New York Regents exam so he could apply for admission to Columbia University. After passing the examination, he received a full-tuition scholarship ($250 per year) to Columbia (Adler, 1977).

At the end of his senior year in 1923, Adler received a note from Dean Hawkes saying that he could attend the commencement exercises but would not receive his bachelor's degree. Because of his aversion to physical education, Adler had not passed his swimming test nor fulfilled the physical education requirement for graduation (1977).

Adler was permitted to enter the graduate school without a B.A. degree and six years later received a Ph.D. in psychology without bothering to receive an M.A. degree. In his autobiography, Adler stressed that he "received" a Ph.D. instead of "earning" it. He hired a student to do the scoring and statistical computations related to his experiment, while another student was paid to construct the graphs and charts for his dissertation. The actual dissertation was written by Adler during a twenty-hour period between 9:00 A.M. one day and 5:00 A.M. the next. During the oral examination that followed, the chairperson noticed from Adler's records that he had not passed his French and German examinations. The chairperson decided to administer a language exam immediately. Adler was asked in French what time it was and in German how he felt. Upon answering these questions, the chairperson declared that he had passed the examination. Adler acknowledged that he might be the only Ph.D. in the country without a master's degree, a bachelor's degree, or even a high school diploma (1977).

Professional Accomplishments

Adler became a teacher in the psychology department at Columbia University in 1923. He had hoped to eventually transfer to Columbia's philosophy department, but he so angered John Dewey while reading a paper for the philosophy department that Dewey got up and left the room muttering that he was not going to listen to someone tell him how to think about God. Adler knew he would have to transfer to another university to realize his dream of teaching in a philosophy department (Adler, 1977).

In 1930, he left Columbia to assume a position in the philosophy department at the University of Chicago. Adler and the president of the University of Chicago, Robert Hutchins, team-taught a seminar course in honors English in the classics, using Socratic dialogue, which later led to Adler's development of the Great Books program. Professor Adler had been Director of the Institute of

Philosophical Research since 1952. He served as the Director of Editorial Planning of the fifteenth edition of Encyclopedia Britannica, and had been Chairman of the Board of Editors since 1974. Since 1945, he had been Associate Editor of the Great Books of the Western World and in 1952 developed its Syntopicon (Rich, 1992, p. 39). In 1988, Adler began serving as a professor at the University of North Carolina at Chapel Hill (McCall, 1994).

Religious Background

Adler's parents were Jewish, but as an adult, he never claimed the Jewish faith as his own. He felt strong ties to Catholicism because of his extensive study of Thomas Aquinas' writings (Clark, 1993).

In his autobiography, written in 1977, Adler shared why he was reluctant to join the Catholic Church. Although Adler had a strong belief in God and viewed Him as the creator of the world, he acknowledged that he did not have a personal relationship with God (1977). In 1980, Adler wrote a book entitled, *How to Think About God*, but he wrote it as an unbeliever (Clark, 1993).

In March of 1984, Adler visited Mexico where he was smitten by a virus. Arriving back in the United States, he spent several weeks in the hospital. During this time, he became deeply depressed. A local pastor began to visit him regularly and shared the Gospel with him. Adler described in detail the night he was miraculously converted to Christianity. He acknowledged a saving faith in Jesus Christ and was ecstatic about the love he felt from God for the first time in his life (Clark, 1993).

The Paideia Proposal

Adler was a major expositor of Aristotle and Aquinas. The primary examples of Adler's interest in Aristotle and Aquinas are exemplified in his books, *Saint Thomas and the Gentiles* (1938) and *Problems for Thomist* (1940). He held Aquinas in high esteem for providing insight regarding Aristotle's writings.

Mortimer Adler was a perennialist. Perennialism is a philosophy founded on the belief that important knowledge that has endured through time should form the basis for a student's education. Perennialism holds that truth is absolute, and it is the task of education to impart these truths. Adler believed that these truths could be found in great books, specifically western classical literature. Truth is the same everywhere and can be discovered by rational beings. Therefore, all students should study the same curriculum.

Adler supported this contention in his book, *The Paideia Proposal,* published in 1982 on behalf of the twenty-two members of the Paideia group.

> "Paideia" (py-dee-a) comes from the Greek pais, paidos: the upbringing of a child. (Related to pedagogy and pediatrics.) In an extended sense, the equivalent of the Latin humanitas (from which "the humanities"), signifying the general learning that should be the possession of all human beings (Adler, 1982, v).

The twenty-two members of the group were teachers, professors, administrators, and authors. They chose to use a philosophical approach instead of conducting a study out in the schools. The 84-page proposal was addressed to Americans who were concerned with the future of the public schools. The Paideia Group called for reforms that could be achieved at the community level, without resorting to a monolithic, national educational system.

Purpose of School

If democracy is to prevail in this country, the Group called for a quality education for all students. Why must a quality education be offered to all? For the proper working of our political institutions, for the efficiency of our industries and businesses, for the salvation of our economy, for the vitality of our culture, and for the ultimate good of our citizens as individuals, and especially our future citizens, our children. (Adler, 1982, p. 4)

In order to achieve quality education for all, Adler proposed a one-track system of schooling, not a system with two or more tracks. A one-track system of public education for twelve years must accomplish three main objectives. The first is called personal growth or self-improvement—mental, moral, and spiritual. Schooling must prepare students to take advantage of all opportunities that society offers.

The second main objective is to prepare students to become enfranchised citizens of this republic. We cannot have a true democracy without universal public schooling. This country cannot afford an ignorant electorate. Students must be prepared to discharge the duties and responsibilities of citizenship.

The third main objective takes account that adults must be able to earn a living. Schooling should not train them for a particular job; it must give them the basic skills that are common to all work in our society (Adler, 1982).

Curriculum

All specialized courses or elective courses should be eliminated. Adler believed that these type of courses were appropriate for colleges or technical schools, but should never be taught in high school. Adler proposed that the same course of study would be required of every student during the twelve years of basic schooling. The only exception would be the inclusion of allowing students to study a foreign language if they so desired.

Adler (1982) believed that the mind could be improved by three different modes:

1. by the acquisition of organized knowledge;

2. by the development of intellectual skills; and

3. by the enlargement of understanding, insight, and aesthetic appreciation.

As a subset of "Acquisition of Knowledge" Adler (1982) listed three areas of subject matter of utmost importance to basic schooling:

1. language, literature, and fine arts;

2. mathematics and natural sciences; and

3. history, geography, and social studies.

Adler (1982) also advocated three auxiliary subjects: physical education for all twelve years, manual arts for several years but not all twelve, and an introduction to the world of work with its range of occupations and careers. The course on the world of work would be taught during the last two years of high school.

Table 3 provides an overview of the three distinct modes of teaching and learning, rising in gradations of complexity and difficulty from the first to twelfth year. All three modes are essential to the overall curriculum (Adler, 1982, p. 23).

Column One: Acquisition of Knowledge

The mode of instruction or the teaching methods for the acquisition of knowledge Adler called "didactic," or "teaching by telling."Textbooks and other instructional materials are to be used along with laboratory demonstrations and experiments. The mind is improved by the acquisition of organized knowledge.

The three columns do not correspond to separate courses, nor is one kind of teaching and learning necessarily confined to any one class.

Language

Instruction in language involves learning of grammar and syntax, the forms of discourse, and the history of the English language.

Mathematics

Instruction in mathematics should begin with simple arithmetic in first grade and rise to at least one year of calculus. The use of calculators and computers should be integrated within the mathematics program.

Science

Students must receive instruction in physics, chemistry, and biology at the secondary level. The interconnectedness and interdependence of these subjects must be stressed. Science instruction at the elementary level must be presented less formally and in a variety of attractive ways.

History

History and geography must include our knowledge of human and social affairs, not only within the boundaries of our nation, but with regard to the world. Preparation for the formal study of history must begin in the early grades by using story-telling and biographical narratives. However, when formal study begins, it must be sequential and systematic, combining a narration of events with information regarding social, political, and economic institutions.

The innovative aspect of the first column is not related to the choice of subject matter but in concentration and continuity of the area being studied. The knowledge offered to a large majority of our high school graduates is inadequate and fragmentary.

Column Two: Development of Skills

Adler stressed the importance of linguistic, mathematical, and scientific skills. He listed reading, writing, speaking, listening, observing, measuring, estimating, and calculating. They are the skills that everyone needs in order to learn anything, in school or elsewhere. Without these skills, it is impossible to learn by one's self, whether for pleasure or work-related activities.

Since what is learned here is skill in performance, not knowledge of facts, the style of teaching cannot be didactic. Telling, demonstrating, or lecturing by the teacher will not suffice for skill development. The teacher must perform as a coach by helping the learner to *do*, to go through the correct motions, and to organize acts in the correct, sequential order. The teacher, like a coach, must be willing to correct faulty performance over and over again until a measure of perfection has been achieved. Only in this way can the ability to think critically—to judge and be discerning—be developed.

Adler argued that Column Two is the backbone of basic schooling. Proficiency in the skills listed is indispensable to the efficient teaching and learning of subject matters in Column One; and it is also necessary for the teaching and learning in Column Three.

Column Three: Enlargement of the Understanding

Adler contends that the mode of teaching espoused in Column Three has all too rarely been attempted in the public schools. The mode of learning in Column Three engages the mind in the study of books (never textbooks) and individual works of merit, accompanied by a discussion of the ideas, values, and the forms presented in the specific work. The appropriate mode of instruction in Column Three is neither didactic nor coaching. It must be the Socratic style of teaching, a mode called *maieutic*, which is a Greek word for midwife, because it assists the student to bring ideas to birth. It is teaching by asking questions, by leading discussions, and by helping students to be raised to a new level of understanding or appreciation.

The interrogative or discussion method of teaching stimulates the imagination and intellect by arousing the creative and inquisitive powers within students, which helps to develop their appreciation of cultural objects.

The books in Column Three—fiction, poetry, essays, history, science, and philosophy—serve a twofold purpose. Discussion draws on the student's skills of reading, writing, speaking, and listening, and uses them to enhance the ability to think clearly, critically, and reflectively. It engages students in disciplined conversation about values and ideas. It also introduces students to the basic ideas in subject matters of Column One.

In addition to knowledge, skills, and understanding, Adler believed that young people need physical education for all twelve years. Also, students could participate in various intramural sports and athletic exercises. Adler also would encourage boys and girls to participate in a wide variety of manual activities such as home economics and woodworking but these courses should *not* be viewed as vocational training. Adler is adamant that vocational training should only occur after the high school experience. He stated that vocational training at the high school level minimized opportunities and was highly undemocratic.

The Role of the Teacher

The establishment of common objectives and well-devised courses of study are the essentials of a basic schooling for all. However, they are only external prerequisites. They are the outer structure, not the heart of the matter. "The heart of the matter is the quality of the learning that goes on during the hours spent in class and during the time spent doing assigned homework" (Adler, 1982, p. 49).

Adler summarized quality learning with the following statements:

> The quality of learning, in turn, depends very largely on the quality of teaching—teaching that guides and inspires learning in the classroom, and that directs and motivates learning to be done homework. Largely but not entirely! Effective learning often occurs in spite of defective teaching. Teaching at its best is only an aid to learning, but that aid is most needed by those who are least adept at learning.
>
> All genuine learning is active, not passive. It involves the use of the mind, not just the memory. It is a process of discovery, in which the student is the main agent, not the teacher.
>
> How does a teacher aid discovery and elicit the activity of the student's mind? By inviting and entertaining questions, by encouraging and sustaining inquiry, by supervising helpfully a wide variety of exercises and drills, by leading discussions, by giving examinations that arouse constructive responses, not just the making of check marks on printed forms. (1982, p. 50)

Adler believed that "learning by discovery can occur without help, but only geniuses can educate themselves without the help of teachers." Teachers must be involved in the process of learning by discovery, but not by attempting to "put" their knowledge into the minds of their students.

Role of the Student

Adler believed that the student must be willing to practice the exercise of learning just like a dedicated athlete might. He stated:

The most important kind of doing, so far as learning is concerned, is intellectual or mental doing. In other words, one can learn to read or write well only by reading and writing, one can learn to measure and calculate well only by measuring and calculating, just as one learns to swim or run well only by swimming or running. (1982, p. 52)

Exercising and practicing during after-school hours may well be required to meet the needs of the coaching teacher. When such homework is done, it must be carefully examined and corrected by the teacher. Without that, it comes to nothing. Moreover, parental support of homework is needed to see that it is done effectively. We are the only country in the world that is lax in this respect. (1982, p. 54)

Summary

This section presented a brief overview of Mortimer Adler's life and his impact on American education. In addition to being a prolific writer and famous philosopher, Adler was well known for his educational manifesto entitled, *The Paideia Proposal*. Adler and his colleagues contended (1) that all students should study the same rigorous, single-track curriculum, (2) that teachers match teaching to students' individual learning styles, and (3) that in every discipline three kinds of teaching and learning are integrated. They are: didactic teaching (lecture), coaching (skill development in small groups with teachers or tutors), and Socratic seminar (a question and discussion process).

Adler died in 2001 at the age of 98.

7

Implementation of the Model and Concluding Remarks

The Challenge of Teaching in a Classical School

During my four-year tenure serving as a headmaster of a private classical and Christian school, the questions raised most often by staff members were related to implementation of the classical model in their classrooms. To state it very bluntly, we as the educators of the school wanted to know, "Are we doing this right?" "What does it really mean to teach classically?" Often times the most insecure teachers regarding their pedagogy were those of us with the most years of teaching experience. We found ourselves mentally juxtaposing our teaching strategies and styles we practiced in former non-classical schools with those we were currently using in this new found "classical realm." Sometimes it felt demoralizing because the juxtaposition failed to produce significant differences.

How did we combat this situation? We brought in speakers with outstanding credentials in the field of philosophy who shared their erudition while providing numerous examples of the outstanding accomplishments of students from antiquity. Following such presentations, we felt even more overwhelmed and inadequate. Numerous times, I recall trying to build-up and restore the self-confidence of outstanding teachers who felt they could not possibly meet the challenges of teaching in a classical school.

To my chagrin, I admit using inclusive pronouns in this description for I too, as a teaching-headmaster, asked the same questions. While I was teaching a Bible or mathematics course, were my lessons significantly different from those I taught in prior years at non-classical schools? The tension created by this type of question was not easily reconcilable. If no significant differences emerged, one felt non-classical. However, when differences were discernable, teachers shared with me that they felt guilty for not doing a better job in prior years.

As I have shared in previous chapters, years of graduate study had allowed me to become familiar with the writings of Mortimer Adler and his ideas of what classical education might produce if embraced once again by public schools in this country. However, my years as a teacher and administrator in a classical school made me painfully aware that I lacked a thorough understanding of why classical education had gone through such an extreme decline in this country. If it were so great, why had it almost slipped into oblivion? I also felt woefully unprepared to share with teachers exactly how classical education should be implemented in their classrooms. My teachers were desperately looking for the magic formula to ease the demands of this daunting task, while I would have gladly shared it with them if I could have only found it. Thus, my quest began.

The Sieve of Classical Philosophy

When I initially began to work on this dissertation, I found materials readily available regarding the decline of classical education, as I have shared in a previous chapter. Regarding implementation, it seemed logical to me that the answer could be found by visiting several prominent classical schools and merely observing how the "experts" did it. In doing so, I found that many teachers at these prominent and successful schools were still looking for the answer to the same question. In fact, while conversing with some teachers, they apparently thought I would surely have the answer since I was a headmaster.

Thus, for months the magical formula that would allow for easy implementation of the model eluded me to the extent that I believed I might never find it, but find it I did! Unfortunately, understanding it is certainly not easy.

While sharing a cup of coffee with a headmaster of a prominent classical school I was visiting, we began to discuss the trials, demands, and joys of administering a classical school. In the course of our conversation, he commented that classical education certainly is about ancient literature, the study of Latin, and using the tools of the trivium. But what is really equates with is a "state of mind" developed through an ongoing understanding of the philosophy of classical education.

As I continued my research throughout the next year, I often thought of his statement. As the concept of classical education became clearer to me, I realized that for me this was the result of beginning to see the "big picture' of classical education. By possessing this "state of mind," we could properly evaluate our own teaching and that of others. What would enable us to do this—our philosophy of education.

The bottom line is that teachers should not wait for the magical pedagogical formula to be presented to them for implementation. We must become active seekers of the truth wherever it might be found. We must use our God-given abilities to motivate and instill passion within our students so that they truly can become life-long learners, equipped to serve their God by serving humanity. We must accomplish this through whatever means are necessary—provided these means are embraced by the classical philosophy of education.

For example, when I was teaching fifth grade back in the '80s, I knew that it was essential for my students to have an understanding of sentence structure. I believed that it was imperative that they understood the components of a sentence and its parts of speech, but I had to battle for the right to share these concepts. The philosophy of "creative writing" that was so in vogue during this time did not allow for such frivolity. Somehow informing a student that he had used the wrong pronoun as the direct object might do immeasurable damage to his self-esteem and stifle his natural desire to write. Come to think of it however, he would not have known what a pronoun was anyway.

Although this might seem to be an example of great hyperbole, it truly is not. Our school's curriculum guide dictated that the parts of speech could not formally be taught until middle school. Intrinsically I knew there was something wrong with this approach, but I lacked the philosophical background to adequately argue my position. What I found out later was that this rule prohibiting the teaching of the parts of speech was not long standing; it had recently been imposed as a result of progressivism re-asserting itself again under the guise of open education.

Those of us in classical schools, who have experienced the joy of teaching Latin to third graders, know how readily students at this age grasp the elements of sentence structure. The study of Latin not only provides another opportunity to elaborate on the rules of grammar, it also provides a direct correlation with improving the skills of English. For those of us in education who have served as athletic coaches, teaching a subject without sharing the rules borders on being ludicrous. John Wooden's maxim of sharing the rules, demonstrating techniques, evaluating the techniques of his players, and providing for hours of practice is applicable to more than the world of college basketball.

As an example related to appropriate content, I share the following story. During my first year as a classical school headmaster, a teacher sought out my advice regarding whether another teacher's bulletin board was appropriate in a classical school. Expecting something controversial, I went to check it out. What I saw was a bulletin board for news items, including a section for sports coverage. Being puzzled, I sought out the former teacher to inquire as to what was her concern. She shared that her understanding was that a classical school had no time for discussing modern-day athletics. If sports were to be discussed it should be limited to only those of ancient Greece. Ultimately, through further discussion, I became aware that her understanding of classical education was almost exclusively related to content—classical meant "old."

Today my only concern about this specific example might be related to the teaching of history. Unfortunately, in many elementary schools today, the teaching of history does not exist; it has been overridden by the teaching of social studies, with some teachers doing very little more than discussing world events on occasion.

Another pertinent example can be illustrated by sharing a story related to "subject integration." The new "middle school philosophy" of the late '80s and '90s bemoaned the isolation of a subject approach to education and actively pushed for an integrated methodology. From my Christian perspective, this approach sounded credible at the time, for I had often shared with my students that the joy of studying came from knowing that we were investigating and coming to a better understanding of God's creation through every area of study. If this approach could help me share the relatedness of God's creation, I would readily employ it.

Unfortunately, what I witnessed over time was that under the guise of integration, entire subjects began to disappear. As a lover of teaching history and literature, I found that integrating the two produced exceptional results. For example, when we studied the American Revolution in history class, we also read the related children's classic, *Johnny Tremain*. As a lover of biographies, I often shared what two or three books I was reading at any given time with the hope that my passion for learning would motivate my students as well. Anecdotally speaking, my intentions were successful, with year after year the school librarian excitedly sharing how many more biographies my students had checked out than other classes.

However, I digress. What was the downside of integration? The answer is that I saw some teachers using the methodology as an excuse to avoid teaching areas of less concern to them. Instead of using *Johnny Tremain* as an integral supplement to their history class, the novel became the class with the systematic teaching of history being avoided. I was guilty at times as well—preferring to share a biography of a given scientist as compared to actually taking the time to set up experiments and make science come to life for my students.

Final Comments

My quest for greater understanding of classical education has taken me on an exciting journey that I hope never ends. Having always been in awe of those possessing expertise in the area of philosophy, I must admit that after spending almost two years devoting myself to reading the "masters," I have even greater respect for those who have dedicated their lives to the study of philosophy.

My hope and prayer is that this dissertation will aid in enabling dedicated educators to become discerning regarding the implementation of classical education in their classrooms. Let me conclude with this example illustrating the importance of developing a classical philosophy of education.

Before I became a teacher, some 27 years ago, I spent countless hours in greenhouses, while growing up on our family produce farm. Early each spring, we would germinate celery in our greenhouses prior to transplanting it outdoors when the weather warmed. Periodically, as part of this process, we found it necessary to bring in fresh soil to help provide the best environment possible for these fledgling seedlings.

Although the soil looked dark and very rich, the first step in preparing this new soil was to process it through a sieve, which was simply a frame with a bottom of fine wire mesh. As the sieve oscillated, the rich and productive soil worked through it, while the unnecessary and foreign objects such as small stones remained in the sieve.

My desire is that this book will help create within you a philosophy of classical education that will function as your sieve—allowing what is good, true, and beautiful to flow from your teaching, thus nurturing and developing your young fledgling students.

Many years ago our family went to see Michael J. Fox's movie *Back to the Future*. Our son, who has a deeply inquisitive nature, was sorely troubled by the movie's title. How could we go "back" to the future? For those of us interested in improving American education, we must struggle with this same concept. Should we venture back in time hundreds of years to embrace an educational philosophy that American schools have discarded?

The answer is yes and no! Please allow me to elaborate. The medieval system of education provided an outstanding education for the students of that time. Is it sufficient for today? Of course not! We live in a world that is dramatically different. The courses of the quadrivium would be woefully inadequate today. Great advances have been made in science, technology, and literature. These areas must be included in a modern-day liberal arts education.

However, is the trivium still as important today as it was then? Absolutely! We must produce high school graduates who have been taught the tools of the trivium. My emphasis is on taught. The educators of today must think of themselves as teachers, not facilitators as prescribed by the progressive movement. To be an educator today, we must commit ourselves to actively teaching these invaluable tools.

I cannot minimize how arduous this task will be. It will take tremendous work and commitment from teachers, students, and parents. However, we keep in mind that the students we teach today will become the leaders of tomorrow. How well they perform that task will depend on how fully we embrace these coveted tools and are willing to impart them to the next generation.

Sayers finished her essay by saying that the purpose of education is to teach students to learn for themselves and any instruction that fails to accomplish this is an effort spent in vain. Through the work of Doug Wilson and thousands of others across this country, we have truly "recovered" these tools. Let us endeavor with all our heart, soul, and mind to pass on this great illuminating torch.

Table 1: Cassiodorus' Topics of Study from:
An Introduction to Divine and Human Readings

1. On the Octateuch

2. On Kings

3. On the Prophets

4. On the Psalter

5. On Solomon

6. On the Hagiographa

7. On the Gospels

8. On the Epistles of the Apostles

9. On the Acts of the Apostles and the Apocalypse

10. On the Modes of Understanding

11. On the Four Accepted Synods

12. The Division of the Divine Scripture According to Jerome

13. The Division of the Divine Scripture According to St. Augustine

14. The Division of the Divine Scripture According to the Septuagint

15. The Caution Which One Should Employ in Reading the Heavenly Authority for the Purpose of Correction

16. On the Excellence of the Divine Scripture

17. On Christian Historians

18. On St. Hilary

19. On St. Cyprian

20. On St. Ambrose

21. On St. Jerome

22. On St. Augustine

23. On the Abbot Eugippius and the Abbot Dionysius

24. General Recapitulation: The Zeal with which the Holy Scripture Ought to be Read

25. Cosmographers to be Read by the Monks

26. On the Adding of Critical Marks

27. On Figures of Speech and the Liberal Arts

28. What is Read by Those Who Cannot Enter Upon Philosophical Writings

29. On the Situation of the Monastery of Vivarium and that of Castellum

30. On Scribes and the Remembering of Correct Spelling

31. On Doctors

Table 2. Student-Centered Instruction versus Teacher-Centered Instruction

Characteristic	Student-Centered Schools	Teacher-Centered Schools
Curriculum	Follow, as much as possible, student interests; integrate materials across subject areas	Standards are established for each grade; specific subjects taught separately
Role of the Teacher	Teacher as facilitator of learning: provides resources, helps students plan and follow their own interests, and keeps records of learner' activities	Teacher as leader of class: is responsible for content, leading lessons, recitation, skills seatwork, and assigning homework
Materials	A rich variety of learning materials, including manipulatives, are used	Teachers work with commercial textbooks
Range of Activities	Use of a wide range of activities based on individual interests	Smaller range of activities, largely teacher-prescribed
Grouping and Teaching Target	Students work in small groups, individually, and/or with teacher guidance based on their own initiative; teaching target is the individual child	Whole class is moved through the same curriculum at roughly the same pace; teacher may teach small groups, especially for beginning reading, provides a degree of indiv. instruction; teaching target is the whole class
Movement	Students are permitted to move around freely and cooperate with other learners	Child-child interactions are restricted
Time	The use of time is flexible, often permitting uninterrupted work sessions largely determined by the learners	The day is divided into distinct periods for teaching different subjects

Evaluation	Based on comparisons of learn-ers with themselves rather than with their classmates or grade standards; preference for diag-nostic rather than norm-refer-enced evaluation	Norm-referenced tests and grade standards; informal and formal testing

(Chall, 2000, p. 29)

Table 3: The Three Columns

	Column One	Column Two	Column Three
Goals	ACQUISITION OF ORGANIZED KNOWLEDGE	DEVELOPMENT OF INTELLECTUAL SKILLS -SKILLS OF LEARNING	ENLARGED UNDERSTANDING OF IDEAS AND VAL- UES
Means	by means of DIDACTIC INSTRUCTION LECTURES AND RESPONSES .... TEXTBOOKS AND OTHER AIDS .... in three areas of	by means of COACHING, EXERCISES AND SUPERVISED PRACTICE in the operations of	by means of MAIEUTIC OR SOCRATIC QUESTIONING AND ACTIVE PARTICIPATION in the
Areas, Operations, and Activities	subject-matter LANGUAGE, LITERATURE AND FINE ARTS .... MATHEMATICS AND NATURAL SCIENCE .... HISTORY, GEOG- RAPHY AND SOCIAL STUDIES	READING, WRITING SPEAKING, LIS- TENING CALCULATING, PROBLEM -SOLVING, OBSERVING, MEA- SURING, ESTIMATING, EXERCISING CRITICAL JUDGMENT	DISCUSSION OF BOOKS (NOT TEXTBOOKS) AND INVOLVEMENT IN ARTISTIC ACTIVITIES e.g., MUSIC, DRAMA, VISUAL ARTS

The three columns do not correspond to separate courses, nor is one kind of teaching and learning necessarily confined to any one class. (Adler, 1982, p. 23)

APPENDIX

The Lost Tools of Learning

In this essay, Miss Sayers suggests that we presently teach our children everything but how to learn. She proposes that we adopt a suitably modified version of the medieval scholastic curriculum for methodological reasons.

"The Lost Tools of Learning" was first presented by Miss Sayers at Oxford in 1947. It is copyrighted by David Higham Associates Ltd., 5-8 Lower John Street, Golden Square, London, UK WIR 4HA and reprinted here with their permission.

I have taken the liberty of adding paragraph numeration as an aid for facilitating discussions.

Introduction

1. That I, whose experience of teaching is extremely limited, should presume to discuss education is a matter, surely, that calls for no apology. It is a kind of behavior to which the present climate of opinion is wholly favorable. Bishops air their opinions about economics; biologists, about metaphysics; inorganic chemists, about theology; the most irrelevant people are appointed to highly technical ministries; and plain, blunt men write to the papers to say that Epstein and Picasso do not know how to draw. Up to a certain point, and provided that the criticisms are made with a reasonable modesty, these activities are commendable. Too much specialization is not a good thing. There is also one excellent reason why the veriest amateur may feel entitled to have an opinion about education. For if we are not all professional teachers, we have all, at some time or another, been taught. Even if we learnt nothing—perhaps in particular if we learnt nothing—our contribution to the discussion may have a potential value.

2. However, it is in the highest degree improbable that the reforms I propose will ever be carried into effect. Neither the parents, nor the training colleges, nor the examination boards, nor the boards of governors, nor the ministries of education, would countenance them for a moment. For they amount to this: that if we are to produce a society of educated people, fitted to preserve their intellectual freedom amid the complex pressures of our modern society, we must turn back the wheel of progress some four or five hundred years, to the point at which education began to lose sight of its true object, towards the end of the Middle Ages.

3. Before you dismiss me with the appropriate phrase—reactionary, romantic, mediaevalist, laudator temporis acti (praiser of times past), or whatever tag comes first to hand—I will ask you to consider one or two miscellaneous questions that hang about at the back, perhaps, of all our minds, and occasionally pop out to worry us.

4. When we think about the remarkably early age at which the young men went up to university in, let us say, Tudor times, and thereafter were held fit to assume responsibility for the conduct of their own affairs, are we altogether comfortable about that artificial prolongation of intellectual childhood and adolescence into the years of physical maturity which is so marked in our own day? To postpone the acceptance of responsibility to a late date brings with it a number of psychological complications which, while they may interest the psychiatrist, are scarcely beneficial either to the individual or to society. The stock argument in favor of postponing the school-leaving age and prolonging the period of education generally is there is now so much more to learn than there was in the Middle Ages. This is partly true, but not wholly. The modern boy and girl are certainly taught more subjects—but does that always mean that they actually know more?

5. Has it ever struck you as odd, or unfortunate, that today, when the proportion of literacy throughout Western Europe is higher than it has ever been, people should have become susceptible to the influence of advertisement and mass propaganda to an extent hitherto unheard of and unimagined? Do you put this down to the mere mechanical fact that the press and the radio and so on have made propaganda much easier to distribute over a wide area? Or do you sometimes have an uneasy suspicion that the product of modern educational methods is less good than he or she might be at disentangling fact from opinion and the proven from the plausible?

6. Have you ever, in listening to a debate among adult and presumably responsible people, been fretted by the extraordinary inability of the average debater to speak to the question, or to meet and refute the arguments of speakers on the other side? Or have you ever pondered upon the extremely high incidence of irrelevant matter which crops up at committee meetings, and upon the very great rarity of persons capable of acting as chairmen of committees? And when you think of this, and think that most of our public affairs are settled by debates and committees, have you ever felt a certain sinking of the heart?

7. Have you ever followed a discussion in the newspapers or elsewhere and noticed how frequently writers fail to define the terms they use? Or how often, if one man does define his terms, another will assume in his reply that he was using the terms in precisely the opposite sense to that in which he has already defined them? Have you ever been faintly troubled by the amount of slipshod syntax going about? And, if so, are you troubled because it is inelegant or because it may lead to dangerous misunderstanding?

8. Do you ever find that young people, when they have left school, not only forget most of what they have learnt (that is only to be expected), but forget also, or betray that they have never really known, how to tackle a new subject for themselves? Are you often bothered by coming across grown-up men and women who seem unable to distinguish between a book that is sound, scholarly, and properly documented, and one that is, to any trained eye, very conspicuously none of these things? Or who cannot handle a library catalogue? Or who, when faced with a book of reference, betray a curious inability to extract from it the passages relevant to the particular question which interests them?

9. Do you often come across people for whom, all their lives, a "subject" remains a "subject," divided by watertight bulkheads from all other "subjects," so that they experience very great difficulty in making an immediate mental connection between let us say, algebra and detective fiction, sewage disposal and the price of salmon—or, more generally, between such spheres of knowledge as philosophy and economics, or chemistry and art?

10. Are you occasionally perturbed by the things written by adult men and women for adult men and women to read? We find a well-known biologist writing in a weekly paper to the effect that: "It is an argument against the existence of a Creator" (I think he put it more strongly; but since I have, most unfortunately, mislaid the reference, I will put his claim at its lowest)—"an argument against the

existence of a Creator that the same kind of variations which are produced by natural selection can be produced at will by stock breeders." One might feel tempted to say that it is rather an argument for the existence of a Creator. Actually, of course, it is neither; all it proves is that the same material causes (recombination of the chromosomes, by crossbreeding, and so forth) are sufficient to account for all observed variations—just as the various combinations of the same dozen tones are materially sufficient to account for Beethoven's Moonlight Sonata and the noise the cat makes by walking on the keys. But the cat's performance neither proves nor disproves the existence of Beethoven; and all that is proved by the biologist's argument is that he was unable to distinguish between a material and a final cause.

11. Here is a sentence from no less academic a source than a front-page article in the Times Literary Supplement: "The Frenchman, Alfred Epinas, pointed out that certain species (e.g., ants and wasps) can only face the horrors of life and death in association." I do not know what the Frenchman actually did say; what the Englishman says he said is patently meaningless. We cannot know whether life holds any horror for the ant, nor in what sense the isolated wasp which you kill upon the window-pane can be said to "face" or not to "face" the horrors of death. The subject of the article is mass behavior in man; and the human motives have been unobtrusively transferred from the main proposition to the supporting instance. Thus the argument, in effect, assumes what it set out to prove—a fact which would become immediately apparent if it were presented in a formal syllogism. This is only a small and haphazard example of a vice which pervades whole books—particularly books written by men of science on metaphysical subjects.

12. Another quotation from the same issue of the TLS comes in fittingly here to wind up this random collection of disquieting thoughts—this time from a review of Sir Richard Livingstone's "Some Tasks for Education": "More than once the reader is reminded of the value of an intensive study of at least one subject, so as to learn 'the meaning of knowledge' and what precision and persistence is needed to attain it. Yet there is elsewhere full recognition of the distressing fact that a man may be master in one field and show no better judgment than his neighbor anywhere else; he remembers what he has learnt, but forgets altogether how he learned it."

13. I would draw your attention particularly to that last sentence, which offers an explanation of what the writer rightly calls the "distressing fact" that the intellectual skills bestowed upon us by our education are not readily transferable to sub-

jects other than those in which we acquired them: "he remembers what he has learnt, but forgets altogether how he learned it."

14. Is not the great defect of our education today—a defect traceable through all the disquieting symptoms of trouble that I have mentioned—that although we often succeed in teaching our pupils "subjects," we fail lamentably on the whole in teaching them how to think: they learn everything, except the art of learning. It is as though we had taught a child, mechanically and by rule of thumb, to play "The Harmonious Blacksmith" upon the piano, but had never taught him the scale or how to read music; so that, having memorized "The Harmonious Blacksmith," he still had not the faintest notion how to proceed from that to tackle "The Last Rose of Summer." Why do I say, "as though"? In certain of the arts and crafts, we sometimes do precisely this—requiring a child to "express himself" in paint before we teach him how to handle the colors and the brush. There is a school of thought which believes this to be the right way to set about the job. But observe: it is not the way in which a trained craftsman will go about to teach himself a new medium. He, having learned by experience the best way to economize labor and take the thing by the right end, will start off by doodling about on an odd piece of material, in order to "give himself the feel of the tool."

Mediaeval Syllabus of the Trivium

15. Let us now look at the mediaeval scheme of education—the syllabus of the Schools. It does not matter, for the moment, whether it was devised for small children or for older students, or how long people were supposed to take over it. What matters is the light it throws upon what the men of the Middle Ages supposed to be the object and the right order of the educative process.

16. The syllabus was divided into two parts: the Trivium and Quadrivium. The second part—the Quadrivium—consisted of "subjects," and need not for the moment concern us. The interesting thing for us is the composition of the Trivium, which preceded the Quadrivium and was the preliminary discipline for it. It consisted of three parts: Grammar, Dialectic, and Rhetoric, in that order.

17. Now the first thing we notice is that two at any rate of these "subjects" are not what we should call "subjects" at all: they are only methods of dealing with subjects. Grammar, indeed, is a "subject" in the sense that it does mean definitely learning a language—at that period it meant learning Latin. But language itself is simply the medium in which thought is expressed. The whole of the Trivium was, in fact, intended to teach the pupil the proper use of the tools of learning,

before he began to apply them to "subjects" at all. First, he learned a language; not just how to order a meal in a foreign language, but the structure of a language, and hence of language itself—what it was, how it was put together, and how it worked. Secondly, he learned how to use language; how to define his terms and make accurate statements; how to construct an argument and how to detect fallacies in argument. Dialectic, that is to say, embraced Logic and Disputation. Thirdly, he learned to express himself in language—how to say what he had to say elegantly and persuasively.

18. At the end of his course, he was required to compose a thesis upon some theme set by his masters or chosen by himself, and afterwards to defend his thesis against the criticism of the faculty. By this time, he would have learned—or woe betide him—not merely to write an essay on paper, but to speak audibly and intelligibly from a platform, and to use his wits quickly when heckled. There would also be questions, cogent and shrewd, from those who had already run the gauntlet of debate.

Modern Syllabus of Subjects

19. It is, of course, quite true that bits and pieces of the mediaeval tradition still linger, or have been revived, in the ordinary school syllabus of today. Some knowledge of grammar is still required when learning a foreign language—perhaps I should say, "is again required," for during my own lifetime, we passed through a phase when the teaching of declensions and conjugations was considered rather reprehensible, and it was considered better to pick these things up as we went along. School debating societies flourish; essays are written; the necessity for "self-expression" is stressed, and perhaps even over-stressed. But these activities are cultivated more or less in detachment, as belonging to the special subjects in which they are pigeon-holed rather than as forming one coherent scheme of mental training to which all "subjects" stand in a subordinate relation. "Grammar" belongs especially to the "subject" of foreign languages, and essay-writing to the "subject" called "English"; while Dialectic has become almost entirely divorced from the rest of the curriculum, and is frequently practiced unsystematically and out of school hours as a separate exercise, only very loosely related to the main business of learning. Taken by and large, the great difference of emphasis between the two conceptions holds good: modern education concentrates on "teaching subjects," leaving the method of thinking, arguing, and expressing one's conclusions to be picked up by the scholar as he goes along' mediaeval education concentrated on first forging and learning to handle the tools of learning,

using whatever subject came handy as a piece of material on which to doodle until the use of the tool became second nature.

20. "Subjects" of some kind there must be, of course. One cannot learn the theory of grammar without learning an actual language, or learn to argue and orate without speaking about something in particular. The debating subjects of the Middle Ages were drawn largely from theology, or from the ethics and history of antiquity. Often, indeed, they became stereotyped, especially towards the end of the period, and the far-fetched and wire-drawn absurdities of Scholastic argument fretted Milton and provide food for merriment even to this day. Whether they were in themselves any more hackneyed and trivial then the usual subjects set nowadays for "essay writing" I should not like to say: we may ourselves grow a little weary of "A Day in My Holidays" and all the rest of it. But most of the merriment is misplaced, because the aim and object of the debating thesis has by now been lost sight of.

21. A glib speaker in the Brains Trust once entertained his audience (and reduced the late Charles Williams to helpless rage) by asserting that in the Middle Ages it was a matter of faith to know how many archangels could dance on the point of a needle. I need not say, I hope, that it never was a "matter of faith"; it was simply a debating exercise, whose set subject was the nature of angelic substance: were angels material, and if so, did they occupy space? The answer usually adjudged correct is, I believe, that angels are pure intelligences; not material, but limited, so that they may have location in space but not extension. An analogy might be drawn from human thought, which is similarly non-material and similarly limited. Thus, if your thought is concentrated upon one thing—say, the point of a needle—it is located there in the sense that it is not elsewhere; but although it is "there," it occupies no space there, and there is nothing to prevent an infinite number of different people's thoughts being concentrated upon the same needle-point at the same time. The proper subject of the argument is thus seen to be the distinction between location and extension in space; the matter on which the argument is exercised happens to be the nature of angels (although, as we have seen, it might equally well have been something else; the practical lesson to be drawn from the argument is not to use words like "there" in a loose and unscientific way, without specifying whether you mean "located there" or "occupying space there."

22. Scorn in plenty has been poured out upon the mediaeval passion for hair-splitting; but when we look at the shameless abuse made, in print and on the

platform, of controversial expressions with shifting and ambiguous connotations, we may feel it in our hearts to wish that every reader and hearer had been so defensively armored by his education as to be able to cry: "Distinguo."

A Plea for Action

23. For we let our young men and women go out unarmed, in a day when armor was never so necessary. By teaching them all to read, we have left them at the mercy of the printed word. By the invention of the film and the radio, we have made certain that no aversion to reading shall secure them from the incessant battery of words, words, words. They do not know what the words mean; they do not know how to ward them off or blunt their edge or fling them back; they are a prey to words in their emotions instead of being the masters of them in their intellects. We who were scandalized in 1940 when men were sent to fight armored tanks with rifles, are not scandalized when young men and women are sent into the world to fight massed propaganda with a smattering of "subjects"; and when whole classes and whole nations become hypnotized by the arts of the spell binder, we have the impudence to be astonished. We dole out lip-service to the importance of education—lip-service and, just occasionally, a little grant of money; we postpone the school-leaving age, and plan to build bigger and better schools; the teachers slave conscientiously in and out of school hours; and yet, as I believe, all this devoted effort is largely frustrated, because we have lost the tools of learning, and in their absence can only make a botched and piecemeal job of it.

A School Based on the Trivium

24. What, then, are we to do? We cannot go back to the Middle Ages. That is a cry to which we have become accustomed. We cannot go back—or can we? Distinguo. I should like every term in that proposition defined. Does "go back" mean a retrogression in time, or the revision of an error? The first is clearly impossible per se; the second is a thing which wise men do every day. "Cannot"—does this mean that our behavior is determined irreversibly, or merely that such an action would be very difficult in view of the opposition it would provoke? Obviously the twentieth century is not and cannot be the fourteenth; but if "the Middle Ages" is, in this context, simply a picturesque phrase denoting a particular educational theory, there seems to be no a priori reason why we should not "go back" to it—with modifications—as we have already "gone back" with modifications, to, let us say, the idea of playing Shakespeare's plays as he wrote them,

and not in the "modernized" versions of Cibber and Garrick, which once seemed to be the latest thing in theatrical progress.

25. Let us amuse ourselves by imagining that such progressive retrogression is possible. Let us make a clean sweep of all educational authorities, and furnish ourselves with a nice little school of boys and girls whom we may experimentally equip for the intellectual conflict along lines chosen by ourselves. We will endow them with exceptionally docile parents; we will staff our school with teachers who are themselves perfectly familiar with the aims and methods of the Trivium; we will have our building and staff large enough to allow our classes to be small enough for adequate handling; and we will postulate a Board of Examiners willing and qualified to test the products we turn out. Thus prepared, we will attempt to sketch out a syllabus—a modern Trivium "with modifications" and we will see where we get to.

26. But first: what age shall the children be? Well, if one is to educate them on novel lines, it will be better that they should have nothing to unlearn; besides, one cannot begin a good thing too early, and the Trivium is by its nature not learning, but a preparation for learning. We will, therefore, "catch 'em young," requiring of our pupils only that they shall be able to read, write, and cipher.

Trivium and Developmental Stages

27. My views about child psychology are, I admit, neither orthodox nor enlightened. Looking back upon myself (since I am the child I know best and the only child I can pretend to know from inside) I recognize three states of development. These, in a rough-and-ready fashion, I will call the Poll-Parrot, the Pert, and the Poetic—the latter coinciding, approximately, with the onset of puberty. The Poll-Parrot stage is the one in which learning by heart is easy and, on the whole, pleasurable; whereas reasoning is difficult and, on the whole, little relished. At this age, one readily memorizes the shapes and appearances of things; one likes to recite the number-plates of cars; one rejoices in the chanting of rhymes and the rumble and thunder of unintelligible polysyllables; one enjoys the mere accumulation of things. The Pert age, which follows upon this (and, naturally, overlaps it to some extent), is characterized by contradicting, answering back, liking to "catch people out" (especially one's elders); and by the propounding of conundrums. Its nuisance-value is extremely high. It usually sets in about the Fourth Form. The Poetic age is popularly known as the "difficult" age. It is self-centered; it yearns to express itself; it rather specializes in being misunderstood; it is restless

and tries to achieve independence; and, with good luck and good guidance, it should show the beginnings of creativeness; a reaching out towards a synthesis of what it already knows, and a deliberate eagerness to know and do some one thing in preference to all others. Now it seems to me that the layout of the Trivium adapts itself with a singular appropriateness to these three ages: Grammar to the Poll-Parrot, Dialectic to the Pert, and Rhetoric to the Poetic age.

Grammar: The Poll-Parrot Years

28. Let us begin, then, with Grammar. This, in practice, means the grammar of some language in particular; and it must be an inflected language. The grammatical structure of an uninflected language is far too analytical to be tackled by any one without previous practice in Dialectic. Moreover, the inflected languages interpret the uninflected, whereas the uninflected are of little use in interpreting the inflected. I will say at once, quite firmly, that the best grounding for education is the Latin grammar. I say this, not because Latin is traditional and mediaeval, but simply because even a rudimentary knowledge of Latin cuts down the labor and pains of learning almost any other subject by at least fifty percent. It is the key to the vocabulary and structure of all the Teutonic languages, as well as to the technical vocabulary of all the sciences and to the literature of the entire Mediterranean civilization, together with all its historical documents.

29. Those whose pedantic preference for a living language persuades them to deprive their pupils of all these advantages might substitute Russian, whose grammar is still more primitive. Russian is, of course, helpful with the other Slav dialects. There is something also to be said for Classical Greek. But my own choice is Latin. Having thus pleased the Classicists among you, I will proceed to horrify them by adding that I do not think it either wise or necessary to cramp the ordinary pupil upon the Procrustean bed of the Augustan Age, with its highly elaborate and artificial verse forms and oratory. Post-classical and mediaeval Latin, which was a living language right down to the end of the Renaissance, is easier and in some ways livelier; a study of it helps to dispel the widespread notion that learning and literature came to a full stop when Christ was born and only woke up again at the Dissolution of the Monasteries.

30. Latin should be begun as early as possible—at a time when inflected speech seems no more astonishing than any other phenomenon in an astonishing world; and when the chanting of "Amo, amas, amat" is as ritually agreeable to the feelings as the chanting of "eeny, meeny, miney, moe."

31. During this age we must, of course, exercise the mind on other things besides Latin grammar. Observation and memory are the faculties most lively at this period; and if we are to learn a contemporary foreign language we should begin now, before the facial and mental muscles become rebellious to strange intonations. Spoken French or German can be practiced alongside the grammatical discipline of the Latin.

32. In English, meanwhile, verse and prose can be learned by heart, and the pupil's memory should be stored with stories of every kind—classical myth, European legend, and so forth. I do not think that the classical stories and masterpieces of ancient literature should be made the vile bodies on which to practice the techniques of Grammar—that was a fault of mediaeval education which we need not perpetuate. The stories can be enjoyed and remembered in English, and related to their origin at a subsequent stage. Recitation aloud should be practiced, individually or in chorus; for we must not forget that we are laying the groundwork for Disputation and Rhetoric.

33. The grammar of History should consist, I think, of dates, events, anecdotes, and personalities. A set of dates to which one can peg all later historical knowledge is of enormous help later on in establishing the perspective of history. It does not greatly matter which dates: those of the Kings of England will do very nicely, provided that they are accompanied by pictures of costumes, architecture, and other everyday things, so that the mere mention of a date calls up a very strong visual presentment of the whole period.

34. Geography will similarly be presented in its factual aspect, with maps, natural features, and visual presentment of customs, costumes, flora, fauna, and so on; and I believe myself that the discredited and old-fashioned memorizing of a few capitol cities, rivers, mountain ranges, etc., does no harm. Stamp collecting may be encouraged.

35. Science, in the Poll-Parrot period, arranges itself naturally and easily around collections—the identifying and naming of specimens and, in general, the kind of thing that used to be called "natural philosophy." To know the name and properties of things is, at this age, a satisfaction in itself; to recognize a devil's coach-horse at sight, and assure one's foolish elders, that, in spite of its appearance, it does not sting; to be able to pick out Cassiopeia and the Pleiades, and perhaps even to know who Cassiopeia and the Pleiades were; to be aware that a whale is not a fish, and a bat not a bird—all these things give a pleasant sensation

of superiority; while to know a ring snake from an adder or a poisonous from an edible toadstool is a kind of knowledge that also has practical value.

36. The grammar of Mathematics begins, of course, with the multiplication table, which, if not learnt now, will never be learnt with pleasure; and with the recognition of geometrical shapes and the grouping of numbers. These exercises lead naturally to the doing of simple sums in arithmetic. More complicated mathematical processes may, and perhaps should, be postponed, for the reasons which will presently appear.

37. So far (except, of course, for the Latin), our curriculum contains nothing that departs very far from common practice. The difference will be felt rather in the attitude of the teachers, who must look upon all these activities less as "subjects" in themselves than as a gathering-together of material for use in the next part of the Trivium. What that material is, is only of secondary importance; but it is as well that anything and everything which can be usefully committed to memory should be memorized at this period, whether it is immediately intelligible or not. The modern tendency is to try and force rational explanations on a child's mind at too early an age. Intelligent questions, spontaneously asked, should, of course, receive an immediate and rational answer; but it is a great mistake to suppose that a child cannot readily enjoy and remember things that are beyond his power to analyze—particularly if those things have a strong imaginative appeal (as, for example, "Kubla Kahn"), an attractive jingle (like some of the memory-rhymes for Latin genders), or an abundance of rich, resounding polysyllables (like the Quicunque vult).

38. This reminds me of the grammar of Theology. I shall add it to the curriculum, because theology is the mistress-science without which the whole educational structure will necessarily lack its final synthesis. Those who disagree about this will remain content to leave their pupil's education still full of loose ends. This will matter rather less than it might, since by the time that the tools of learning have been forged the student will be able to tackle theology for himself, and will probably insist upon doing so and making sense of it. Still, it is as well to have this matter also handy and ready for the reason to work upon. At the grammatical age, therefore, we should become acquainted with the story of God and Man in outline—i.e., the Old and New Testaments presented as parts of a single narrative of Creation, Rebellion, and Redemption—and also with the Creed, the Lord's Prayer, and the Ten Commandments. At this early stage, it does not mat-

ter nearly so much that these things should be fully understood as that they should be known and remembered.

Dialectic: The Pert Years

39. It is difficult to say at what age, precisely, we should pass from the first to the second part of the Trivium. Generally speaking, the answer is: so soon as the pupil shows himself disposed to pertness and interminable argument. For as, in the first part, the master faculties are Observation and Memory, so, in the second, the master faculty is the Discursive Reason. In the first, the exercise to which the rest of the material was, as it were, keyed, was the Latin grammar; in the second, the key-exercise will be Formal Logic. It is here that our curriculum shows its first sharp divergence from modern standards. The disrepute into which Formal Logic has fallen is entirely unjustified; and its neglect is the root cause of nearly all those disquieting symptoms which we have noted in the modern intellectual constitution. Logic has been discredited, partly because we have come to suppose that we are conditioned almost entirely by the intuitive and the unconscious. There is no time to argue whether this is true; I will simply observe that to neglect the proper training of the reason is the best possible way to make it true. Another cause for the disfavor into which Logic has fallen is the belief that it is entirely based upon universal assumptions that are either unprovable or tautological. This is not true. Not all universal propositions are of this kind. But even if they were, it would make no difference, since every syllogism whose major premise is in the form "All A is B" can be recast in hypothetical form. Logic is the art of arguing correctly: "If A, then B." The method is not invalidated by the hypothetical nature of A. Indeed, the practical utility of Formal Logic today lies not so much in the establishment of positive conclusions as in the prompt detection and exposure of invalid inference.

40. Let us now quickly review our material and see how it is to be related to Dialectic. On the Language side, we shall now have our vocabulary and morphology at our fingertips; henceforward we can concentrate on syntax and analysis (i.e., the logical construction of speech) and the history of language (i.e., how we came to arrange our speech as we do in order to convey our thoughts).

41. Our Reading will proceed from narrative and lyric to essays, argument and criticism, and the pupil will learn to try his own hand at writing this kind of thing. Many lessons—on whatever subject—will take the form of debates; and the place of individual or choral recitation will be taken by dramatic perfor-

mances, with special attention to plays in which an argument is stated in dramatic form.

42. Mathematics—algebra, geometry, and the more advanced kinds of arithmetic—will now enter into the syllabus and take its place as what it really is: not a separate "subject" but a sub-department of Logic. It is neither more nor less than the rule of the syllogism in its particular application to number and measurement, and should be taught as such, instead of being, for some, a dark mystery, and, for others, a special revelation, neither illuminating nor illuminated by any other part of knowledge.

43. History, aided by a simple system of ethics derived from the grammar of theology, will provide much suitable material for discussion: Was the behavior of this statesman justified? What was the effect of such an enactment? What are the arguments for and against this or that form of government? We shall thus get an introduction to constitutional history—a subject meaningless to the young child, but of absorbing interest to those who are prepared to argue and debate. Theology itself will furnish material for argument about conduct and morals; and should have its scope extended by a simplified course of dogmatic theology (i.e., the rational structure of Christian thought), clarifying the relations between the dogma and the ethics, and lending itself to that application of ethical principles in particular instances which is properly called casuistry. Geography and the Sciences will likewise provide material for Dialectic.

44. But above all, we must not neglect the material which is so abundant in the pupils' own daily life.

45. There is a delightful passage in Leslie Paul's "The Living Hedge" which tells how a number of small boys enjoyed themselves for days arguing about an extraordinary shower of rain which had fallen in their town—a shower so localized that it left one half of the main street wet and the other dry. Could one, they argued, properly say that it had rained that day on or over the town or only in the town? How many drops of water were required to constitute rain? And so on. Argument about this led on to a host of similar problems about rest and motion, sleep and waking, est and non est, and the infinitesimal division of time. The whole passage is an admirable example of the spontaneous development of the ratiocinative faculty and the natural and proper thirst of the awakening reason for the definition of terms and exactness of statement. All events are food for such an appetite.

46. An umpire's decision; the degree to which one may transgress the spirit of a regulation without being trapped by the letter: on such questions as these, children are born casuists, and their natural propensity only needs to be developed and trained—and especially, brought into an intelligible relationship with the events in the grown-up world. The newspapers are full of good material for such exercises: legal decisions, on the one hand, in cases where the cause at issue is not too abstruse; on the other, fallacious reasoning and muddleheaded arguments, with which the correspondence columns of certain papers one could name are abundantly stocked.

47. Wherever the matter for Dialectic is found, it is, of course, highly important that attention should be focused upon the beauty and economy of a fine demonstration or a well-turned argument, lest veneration should wholly die. Criticism must not be merely destructive; though at the same time both teacher and pupils must be ready to detect fallacy, slipshod reasoning, ambiguity, irrelevance, and redundancy, and to pounce upon them like rats. This is the moment when precise-writing may be usefully undertaken; together with such exercises as the writing of an essay, and the reduction of it, when written, by 25 or 50 percent.

48. It will, doubtless, be objected that to encourage young persons at the Pert age to browbeat, correct, and argue with their elders will render them perfectly intolerable. My answer is that children of that age are intolerable anyhow; and that their natural argumentativeness may just as well be canalized to good purpose as allowed to run away into the sands. It may, indeed, be rather less obtrusive at home if it is disciplined in school; and anyhow, elders who have abandoned the wholesome principle that children should be seen and not heard have no one to blame but themselves.

49. Once again, the contents of the syllabus at this stage may be anything you like. The "subjects" supply material; but they are all to be regarded as mere grist for the mental mill to work upon. The pupils should be encouraged to go and forage for their own information, and so guided towards the proper use of libraries and books for reference, and shown how to tell which sources are authoritative and which are not.

50. Towards the close of this stage, the pupils will probably be beginning to discover for themselves that their knowledge and experience are insufficient, and that their trained intelligences need a great deal more material to chew upon. The imagination—usually dormant during the Pert age—will reawaken, and prompt

them to suspect the limitations of logic and reason. This means that they are passing into the Poetic age and are ready to embark on the study of Rhetoric. The
doors of the storehouse of knowledge should now be thrown open for them to
browse about as they will. The things once learned by rote will be seen in new
contexts; the things once coldly analyzed can now be brought together to form a
new synthesis; here and there a sudden insight will bring about that most exciting
of all discoveries: the realization that truism is true.

Rhetoric: The Poetic Years

51. It is difficult to map out any general syllabus for the study of Rhetoric: a certain freedom is demanded. In literature, appreciation should be again allowed to
take the lead over destructive criticism; and self-expression in writing can go forward, with its tools now sharpened to cut clean and observe proportion. Any
child who already shows a disposition to specialize should be given his head: for,
when the use of the tools has been well and truly learned, it is available for any
study whatever. It would be well, I think, that each pupil should learn to do one,
or two, subjects really well, while taking a few classes in subsidiary subjects so as
to keep his mind open to the inter-relations of all knowledge. Indeed, at this
stage, our difficulty will be to keep "subjects" apart; for Dialectic will have shown
all branches of learning to be inter-related, so Rhetoric will tend to show that all
knowledge is one. To show this, and show why it is so, is pre-eminently the task
of the mistress science. But whether theology is studied or not, we should at least
insist that children who seem inclined to specialize on the mathematical and scientific side should be obliged to attend some lessons in the humanities and vice
versa. At this stage, also, the Latin grammar, having done its work, may be
dropped for those who prefer to carry on their language studies on the modern
side; while those who are likely never to have any great use or aptitude for mathematics might also be allowed to rest, more or less, upon their oars. Generally
speaking, whatsoever is mere apparatus may now be allowed to fall into the background, while the trained mind is gradually prepared for specialization in the
"subjects" which, when the Trivium is completed, it should be perfectly will
equipped to tackle on its own. The final synthesis of the Trivium—the presentation and public defense of the thesis—should be restored in some form; perhaps
as a kind of "leaving examination" during the last term at school.

52. The scope of Rhetoric depends also on whether the pupil is to be turned out
into the world at the age of 16 or whether he is to proceed to the university.
Since, really, Rhetoric should be taken at about 14, the first category of pupil

should study Grammar from about 9 to 11, and Dialectic from 12 to 14; his last two school years would then be devoted to Rhetoric, which, in this case, would be of a fairly specialized and vocational kind, suiting him to enter immediately upon some practical career. A pupil of the second category would finish his Dialectical course in his preparatory school, and take Rhetoric during his first two years at his public school. At 16, he would be ready to start upon those "subjects" which are proposed for his later study at the university: and this part of his education will correspond to the mediaeval Quadrivium. What this amounts to is that the ordinary pupil, whose formal education ends at 16, will take the Trivium only; whereas scholars will take both the Trivium and the Quadrivium.

Trivium: Educational Capital

53. Is the Trivium, then, a sufficient education for life? Properly taught, I believe that it should be. At the end of the Dialectic, the children will probably seem to be far behind their coevals brought up on old-fashioned "modern" methods, so far as detailed knowledge of specific subjects is concerned. But after the age of 14 they should be able to overhaul the others hand over fist. Indeed, I am not at all sure that a pupil thoroughly proficient in the Trivium would not be fit to proceed immediately to the university at the age of 16, thus proving himself the equal of his mediaeval counterpart, whose precocity astonished us at the beginning of this discussion. This, to be sure, would make hay of the English public-school system, and disconcert the universities very much. It would, for example, make quite a different thing of the Oxford and Cambridge boat race.

54. But I am not here to consider the feelings of academic bodies: I am concerned only with the proper training of the mind to encounter and deal with the formidable mass of undigested problems presented to it by the modern world. For the tools of learning are the same, in any and every subject; and the person who knows how to use them will, at any age, get the mastery of a new subject in half the time and with a quarter of the effort expended by the person who has not the tools at his command. To learn six subjects without remembering how they were learnt does nothing to ease the approach to a seventh; to have learnt and remembered the art of learning makes the approach to every subject an open door.

55. Before concluding these necessarily very sketchy suggestions, I ought to say why I think it necessary, in these days, to go back to a discipline which we had discarded. The truth is that for the last three hundred years or so we have been living upon our educational capital. The post-Renaissance world, bewildered and

excited by the profusion of new "subjects" offered to it, broke away from the old discipline (which had, indeed, become sadly dull and stereotyped in its practical application) and imagined that henceforward it could, as it were, disport itself happily in its new and extended Quadrivium without passing through the Trivium. But the Scholastic tradition, though broken and maimed, still lingered in the public schools and universities: Milton, however much he protested against it, was formed by it—the debate of the Fallen Angels and the disputation of Abdiel with Satan have the tool-marks of the Schools upon them, and might, incidentally, profitably figure as set passages for our Dialectical studies. Right down to the nineteenth century, our public affairs were mostly managed, and our books and journals were for the most part written, by people brought up in homes, and trained in places, where that tradition was still alive in the memory and almost in the blood. Just so, many people today who are atheist or agnostic in religion, are governed in their conduct by a code of Christian ethics which is so rooted that it never occurs to them to question it.

56. But one cannot live on capital forever. However firmly a tradition is rooted, if it is never watered, though it dies hard, yet in the end it dies. And today a great number—perhaps the majority—of the men and women who handle our affairs, write our books and our newspapers, carry out our research, present our plays and our films, speak from our platforms and pulpits—yes, and who educate our young people—have never, even in a lingering traditional memory, undergone the Scholastic discipline. Less and less do the children who come to be educated bring any of that tradition with them. We have lost the tools of learning—the axe and the wedge, the hammer and the saw, the chisel and the plane—that were so adaptable to all tasks. Instead of them, we have merely a set of complicated jigs, each of which will do but one task and no more, and in using which eye and hand receive no training, so that no man ever sees the work as a whole or "looks to the end of the work."

57. What use is it to pile task on task and prolong the days of labor, if at the close the chief object is left unattained? It is not the fault of the teachers—they work only too hard already. The combined folly of a civilization that has forgotten its own roots is forcing them to shore up the tottering weight of an educational structure that is built upon sand. They are doing for their pupils the work which the pupils themselves ought to do. For the sole true end of education is simply this: to teach men how to learn for themselves; and whatever instruction fails to do this is effort spent in vain.

Recommended Readings

The following are recommended readings for those who would like to explore classical education in greater detail.

Adler, Mortimer, *The Paideia Proposal: An Educational Manifesto,* 1982

- Adler presents his approach for the type of classical education that could be used in public schools.

Adler, Mortimer, *Philosopher at Large: An Intellectual Autobiography,* 1977 and *A Second Look in the Rearview Mirror: A Further Autobiographical Reflections of a Philosopher at Large,* 1992

- In these autobiographies Adler shares about his personal life while also sharing the challenges of his ongoing battle with pragmatism in our country. A proponent of the "Great Books" and classical education, he passed away in 2001 at the age of 98.

Bloom, Allan, *The Closing of the American Mind,* 1987

- Bloom was a professor at the University of Chicago. His book, which laments the decay of humanities in our universities, became a best seller.

Boethius, *The Consolation of Philosophy,* Translated by H.F. Stewart, E.K. Rand, and S.J. Tester, 1918

- Boethius was a Roman statesman who was executed in 524 A.D. While awaiting his death, he wrote this famous treatise of the benefits of philosophy.

Graves, Frank, A History of Education: *During the Middle Ages and the Transition to Modern Times,* 1910

- This book provides a wealth of information concerning the evolution from monastic and cathedral schools to the advent of medieval universities.

Hanson, Victor & Heath, John, Who Killed Homer? *The Demise of Classical Education and the Recovery of Greek Wisdom*, 1998

- Like numerous other authors, they give evidence that classical education is under assault and rapidly disappearing from our American high schools and colleges. Their position is unique in the sense that they place the blame on the shoulders of the university classicists.

Haskins, Charles, *The Rise of Universities*, 1923

- Based on his university lectures, Haskins does an outstanding job of presenting the backdrop for the development of medieval universities.

Hicks, David, *Norms & Nobility: A Treatise on Education*, 1981

- Hicks is the President of the Darlington School in Rome, Georgia. Hicks contends that classical education is not elitist or irrelevant, and can be used to resurrect a spirit of inquiry among our students.

Hirsch, E.D., *Cultural Literacy: What Every American Needs to Know*, 1987

- Hirsch contends that the culture of our country is changing dramatically because we longer share a common bond of basic knowledge. We need these points of reference so that we can communicate adequately with one-another.

Howie, George, *St. Augustine on Education*, 1969

- Howie has translated numerous writings from Augustine related to education and provides explanations and commentary.

Jaeger, Warren, *Paideia: The Ideals of Greek Culture,* translated by Gilbert Highet, 1986

- Jaeger's classic three-volume work was originally published in 1939. Jaeger evaluates Hellenic culture by examining its civilization, tradition, literature, and philosophy.

Joseph, Sister Miriam, *The Trivium: The Liberal Arts of Logic, Grammar, and Rhetoric,* 2002

- Sister Miriam Joseph first brought us this text on the trivium in 1937. It provides definitions and examples of the components of logic and rhetoric.

John of Salisbury, translated by McGarry, Daniel, *The Metalogicon* or *Defense of the Trivium*, 1971

- John of Salisbury was a student of Peter Abelard. For the serious student of classical education, McGarry provides us with a translation of John of Salisbury's important work from the 12th century in defense of the trivium.

Kopff, E. Christian, *The Devil Knows Latin: Why America Needs the Classical Tradition*, 1999

- Kopff is a classicist from the University of Colorado who laments how the decline of Latin and Greek studies in our universities is eroding our liberal arts tradition.

Manville, Brook, and Ober, Josiah, *A Company of Citizens*, 2003

- Manville is a chief learning officer for a software company, and Ober is a professor of classics at Princeton University. They share lessons from Athenian history that may be relevant today regarding organizational structure and managing of people.

Martianus Capella, *The Marriage of Philogy and Mercury*, translated by William Stahl, 1977

- This is a famous and very unique textbook. The seven components of liberal arts are represented as handmaidens who come to attend the wedding of Philogy and Mercury. Their addresses as written by Martianus was used a textbook for centuries.

Morris, Tom, *If Aristotle Ran General Motors: The New Soul of Business*, 1997

- Morris contends that openness and integrity must be part of the workplace. He envisions a workplace where one can truly think about truth, beauty, goodness, and unity if we allow ourselves to be guided by the great thinkers of the past.

Newman, John, The Idea of a University, first published in various editions in the 1850s

- Newman was a Fellow at Oriel and ordained clergyman of the Church of England who later became a Catholic priest. The book consists of a series of lectures he presented at the new Catholic University in Dublin. The all-encompassing idea behind the lectures was that "all knowledge forms one whole" under the governance of theology. He was writing in opposition to the proposal that newly created universities in England would not offer theology classes.

Ravitch, Diane, *The Troubled Crusade*, 1983 and *Left Back*, 2001

- Diane Ravitch is a former assistant secretary of education and a prolific writer on educational reforms. These books deal with the detrimental effects of progressive education during the past 100 years.

Reynolds, Barbara, *Dorothy L. Sayers: Her Life and Soul*, 1993

- Reynolds was a close friend of Sayers and completed Sayers' translation of Dante's *Divine Comedy* following her death. Having unprecedented access to Sayers' personal papers, she writes a balanced portrait of this catalyst for classical education.

Sproul, R.C., *The Consequences of Ideas: Understanding the Concepts That Shaped Our World*, 2000

- Dr. Sproul surveys the history of philosophy to show how the ideas from the philosophers of the past continue to impact our world today.

Veith, Gene Edward and Kern, Andrew, *Classical Education*, 1997

- This book offers insight on classical education as derived from extended visits to Logos School in Moscow, Idaho, and The Geneva School in Orlando, Florida.

Wagner, David L., *The Seven Liberal Arts in the Middle Ages*, 1983

- Wagner is editor of this text that presents essays on the trivium and quadrivium. This text is definitely not for the novice.

Wills, Garry, *St. Augustine's Childhood* and *The Teacher*, 2001

- Wills presents us with a translation of Augustine's book one of his *Confessions*. Also included is a translation of *The Teacher*, a dialogue conducted between Augustine and his son.

Wills, Garry, *Saint Augustine*, 1999

- This short but interesting biography of St. Augustine is part of the Penguin Lives series.

Winterer, Caroline, *The Culture of Classicism: Ancient Greece and Rome in American Intellectual Life from 1780–1910,* 2002

- Should American university students be required to master a common core of knowledge? This book traces the emergence of the classical model that became standard in the American curriculum in the nineteenth century and provides an explanation for its decline.

References

Adler, M. J. (1977). *Philosopher at large: An intellectual autobiography.* New York: Macmillan

Adler, M. J. (1978). *Aristotle for everybody: Difficult thought made easy.* New York: Touchstone

Adler, M. J. (1982). *The paideia proposal: An educational manifesto.* New York: Collier ooks.

Adler, M. J. (1983). *Paideia problems and possibilities.* New York: Collier Books.

Adler, M. J. (1988). *Reforming education* (rev. ed.). New York: Collier Books.

Adler, M. J. (1992). *A second look in the rearview mirror.* New York: Macmillan.

Augustine, A. (1998). *Confessions* (H. Chadwick, Trans.). Oxford: University Press

Bacon, F. (1937). *Advancement of learning.* New York: Odyssey Press

Bogden, R. C., & Biklen, S. K. *Qualitative research for education: An introduction to theory and method* (2nd ed.). Needham Heights, MA: Allyn & Bacon.

Buckley, W.F. (1959). *Up from liberalism.* New York: Stein and Day

Capella, M. (1977). *The marriage of philogy and Mercury* (H.Stahl, Trans.). New York: Columbia University Press

Cassiodorus. (1966). *An introduction to divine and human readings* (L. Jones, Trans.). New York: Octagon Books, Inc.

Chall, J.S. (2000). *The academic achievement challenge: What really works in the classroom?* New York: The Guilford Press

Clark, K. J. (Ed.). (1993). *Philosophers who believe.* Downers Grove: Intervarsity Press.

Creswell, J. W. (1998). *Qualitative inquiry and research design.* Thousand Oaks, CA: Sage Publications

Dahmus, J. (1995). *A history of the Middle Ages.* New York: Barnes and Noble Books

Durant, W. (1926). *The story of philosophy: The lives and opinions of the greater philosophers.* New York: Simon and Schuster

Finn, C. E., & Rebarber, T. (1999). *Education reform in the '90s.* New York: Macmillan Publishing

Elias, J.L. (2002). A history of Christian education: Protestant, Catholic, and orthodox perspectives. Malbar, Florida: Krieger Publishing Company

Ellis, A. K., Cogan, J. J., & Howey, K. R. (1991). *Introduction to the foundations of education* (3rd ed.). Englewood Cliffs: Prentice Hall.

Everitt, A. (2001). Cicero: *The life and times of Rome's greatest politician.* New York: Random House

Gettys, C. M., & Wheelock, A. (1994). Launching Paideia in Chattanooga. *Educational Leadership, 52,* 12-15.

Gottlieb, A. (2000). *The dream of reason: A history of western philosophy from the Greeks to the Renaissance.* New York: W.W. Norton & Company

Graves, F.P. (1910). A history of education: During the middle ages and the transition to modern times. New York: Macmillan Co.

Gutek, G.L. (1972). *A history of western educational experience.* Prospect Heights, Illinois: Waveland Press

Guthrie, J. W., & Reed, R. J. (1991). *Educational administration and policy: Effective leadership for American education* (2nd ed.). Boston: Allyn and Bacon.

Hanson, V.D., & Heath, J. (2001). *Who killed Homer? The demise of classical education and the recovery of Greek wisdom.* San Francisco: Encounter Books

Haskins, C.H. (1923). *The rise of universities.* New York: H. Holt

Howick, W.H. (1971). *Philosophies of western education.* Danville, Illinois: Interstate Printers

Howie, G. (1969). *St. Augustine: On education.* Chicago: Henry Regnery Company

Isocrates. *Ad Nicocles*

Isocrates. *Against the Sophists*

Isocrates. *Antidosis*

John of Salisbury. (1971). The metalogicon (D. McGarry, Trans.). Gloucester, Massachusettes: Peter Smith Publishing

Kennedy, G.A. (1999). *Classical rhetoric & its Christian and secular tradition: From ancient to modern times.* Chapel Hill: The University of North Carolina Press

Locke, J. (1996). Some thoughts concerning education. Indianapolis, Indiana: Hackett Publishing

Locke, J. (1996). Of the conduct of the understanding. Indianapolis, Indiana: Hackett Publishing

McCall, J. (1994). *The principal's edge.* Princeton Junction: Eye on Education.

Merriam, S. (1998). *Qualitative research and case study applications in education.* San Francisco: Jossey-Bass Publishers.

Marrou, H.I. (1956). *A history of education in antiquity* (G. Lamb, Trans.). New York: Sheed & Ward

The National Commission on Excellence in Education. (1984). *A nation at risk: The full account.* Portland: USA Research, Inc.

Piper, J. (2000). *The legacy of sovereign joy: God's triumphant grace in the lives of Augustine, Luther, and Calvin.* Wheaton, Illinois: Crossways Books

Pulliam, J. D., & Van Patten, J. (1995). *History of education in America* (6th ed.). Englewood Cliffs: Merrill.

Quintilian. (1987). *Institutio Oratoria* (J. Murphy, Trans.). Carbondale, Illinois: Southern Illinois University Press

Rich, J. M. (Ed.). (1992). *Innovations in education: Reformers and their critics.* Boston: Allyn and Bacon.

Ross, D. (1996, 1923). *Aristotle.* London: Routledge

Rubenstein, R. (2003). *Aristotle's children: How Christians, Muslims, and Jews rediscovered ancient wisdom and illuminated the dark ages.* Orlando: Harcourt, Inc.

Sayers, D. (1948). *The Lost Tools of Learning.* Methuen

Simmons, T.L. (2002). *Climbing Parnassus: a new apologia for Greek and Latin.* Wilmington, Delaware: ISI Books

Sproul, R.C. (1986). Lifeviews: Understanding the ideas that shape society today. Old Tappan, New Jersey: Fleming H. Revell Company

Sproul, R.C. (2000). *The consequences of ideas: Understanding the concepts that shaped our world.* Wheaton, Illinois: Crossway Books

Van Doren, C. (1991). *A history of knowledge: Past, present, and future.* New York: Ballantine Books

Veatch, H.B. (1974). *Aristotle: A contemporary appreciation.* London: Indiana University Press

Veith, D., & Kern, A. (1997). *Classical education.* Washington, DC: Capital Research Center

Wills, G. (1999). *St. Augustine.* New York: Penguin Group

Wills, G. (2001). *St. Augustine's childhood: Confessiones book one.* New York: Penguin Group

Winterer, C. (2002). *The culture of classicism: Ancient Greece and Rome in American intellectual life, 1780–1910.* Baltimore: The Johns Hopkins University Press

Yin, R. K. (1994). *Case study research: Design and methods* (2nd ed.). Thousand Oaks, CA: Sage.

Index

A

a priori 5, 8, 14, 51, 110
Abelard 40, 42, 44, 45, 52, 53, 54, 55, 123
Academy 13, 14, 17, 18, 22, 41, 82
Adeodatus 32, 35
Adler 1, 4, 5, 20, 21, 57, 82, 83, 84, 85, 86, 87, 88, 89, 90, 92, 101, 121, 127
Alexander the Great 17, 18
Alexandria 38
Alypius 35
Andronicus of Rhodes 19
Anselm 50, 51
Antidosis 22, 23, 129
Apology 11, 103
Aquinas 21, 42, 55, 56, 84
Aristotle 5, 6, 17, 18, 19, 20, 21, 25, 42, 48, 49, 55, 58, 59, 65, 84, 123, 127, 130
arrangement 25
Association of Classical and Christian Schools (ACCS) 82
Augustine 5, 31, 32, 33, 34, 35, 36, 37, 50, 51, 78, 97, 98, 122, 124, 125, 127, 129, 130
axiology 4, 5, 6, 7, 9

B

Bacon 58, 59, 127, 128, 130
Blackwell 74
Bloom 4, 5, 121
Boethius 40, 48, 121
Bologna 41, 43, 44, 45
Bridgeheads 75
Buckley 81, 127

C

Cambridge 45, 46, 47, 59, 119
Capella 39, 47, 123, 127
Cardinal Principles of Secondary Education 69
Carthage 31, 32, 33, 43
Cassiciacum 35
Cassiodorus 31, 38, 39, 40, 97, 127
cathedral schools 42, 48, 121
Chall 69, 100, 127
chanting 35, 37, 111, 112
child-centered 3, 68
Cicero 10, 21, 32, 33, 40, 73, 128
classical education 1, 2, 3, 8, 9, 10, 11, 13, 19, 22, 26, 36, 39, 57, 58, 60, 70, 71, 81, 82, 92, 94, 95, 121, 122, 123, 124, 129, 130
classroom management 3
Clouds of Witness 74
Committee of Ten 69
Confessions 31, 32, 33, 34, 35, 37, 124, 127
Consequences of Ideas 14, 124, 130
Constantinus Africanus 43
Corpus Juris Civilis 43, 44, 49
Cultural Literacy 3, 122
curriculum 2, 5, 7, 21, 22, 36, 37, 46, 47, 48, 49, 52, 68, 69, 84, 86, 90, 93, 99, 103, 108, 114, 115, 125

D

Dante 1, 71, 75, 76, 124
Decretum Gratiani 44
delivery 25, 26
Democracy and Education 67
Descartes 58, 60

Dewey 1, 8, 9, 57, 60, 64, 65, 66, 67, 69, 83

dialectic 16, 25, 39, 44, 71, 79, 80, 107, 108, 112, 115, 116, 117, 118, 119

disputation 48, 50, 108, 113, 120

Divine Comedy 1, 71, 75, 76, 124

Divine Letters 39

dumb ox 55

Duns Scotus 42

Durant 13, 15, 16, 18, 64, 128

E

Edward VIII 75

elocution 25

Emile 61, 62

English 77

Enlightenment 57, 58, 59, 60, 61, 62, 63, 64

epistemology 4, 6, 7, 9, 13

Euclid 42, 48

F

Fleming 74, 75, 130

Froebel 62

G

Galen 49

Geography 77, 78, 80, 86, 87, 101, 113, 116

George V 75

Gilchrist Scholarship 73

Godolphin School 73

Grammar 11, 16, 21, 25, 26, 29, 30, 31, 37, 39, 47, 48, 49, 71, 77, 78, 79, 87, 93, 107, 108, 109, 112, 113, 114, 115, 116, 118, 119, 122

Grammar Stage 16, 37, 77, 79

Grammar Teachers 30

Gratian 44

great conversation 4

Gutek 11, 15, 20, 21, 26, 42, 53, 54, 55, 56, 128

Gymnastics 15, 16, 26

H

Hellenistic Age 2

Heloise 40, 53, 54

Heraclitus 9, 64

Hermeias 17

Hibbert Journal 81

Hippocrates 43, 49

Hirsch 3, 4, 122

History 1, 2, 5, 6, 7, 15, 23, 26, 41, 42, 45, 46, 47, 49, 57, 58, 60, 61, 65, 66, 68, 69, 75, 77, 78, 80, 86, 87, 88, 94, 101, 109, 113, 115, 116, 121, 123, 124, 128, 129, 130

Homer 15, 122, 129

Hortensius 33

Hutchins 5, 21, 83

I

idealism 1, 5, 8, 51, 62

Idealists 4, 5, 23

Institutio oratoria 24, 25, 130

instrumentalism 64, 67

Invention 25, 110

Isocrates 21, 22, 23, 24, 25, 129

J

James 8, 58, 63, 64, 65, 66, 67

John of Salisbury 31, 48, 123, 129

K

Kant 58, 62

Kennedy 22, 129

Knowledge 5, 86

L

Laertius 16

Language 79, 87, 107, 108, 109, 112, 113, 115, 118

Latin 26, 32, 41, 48, 49, 60, 61, 72, 73, 75, 79, 80, 85, 92, 93, 107, 112, 113, 114, 115, 118, 123, 130

Left Back 68, 124

Liberal Arts 2, 7, 20, 21, 26, 37, 38, 39, 43, 47, 49, 55, 57, 69, 96, 98, 122, 123, 124

Life Experiences 80

literature 5, 6, 15, 21, 22, 32, 36, 38, 48, 49, 76, 84, 86, 92, 94, 96, 101, 112, 113, 118, 122

Locke 58, 60, 129

Logic 11, 14, 18, 21, 47, 48, 49, 50, 51, 52, 79, 80, 115, 116, 118, 122

Logic Stage 79

Logos School 82, 124

Lost Tools of Learning 1, 71, 72, 81, 82, 103, 130

Lyceum School 18

M

Mac 76

MAIEUTIC 88, 101

Mani 33

Manicheans 33

Manicheism 33

Marrou 13, 15, 22, 23, 24, 129

Martianus Capella 47, 123

Mathematics 5, 7, 13, 14, 15, 16, 18, 21, 23, 29, 49, 69, 77, 78, 80, 81, 86, 87, 91, 101, 114, 116, 118

memory 25, 26, 28, 61, 89, 113, 114, 115, 120

Metalogicon 48, 123, 129

metaphysics 4, 5, 6, 9, 18, 21, 49, 50, 65, 66, 103

Metaphysics Club 65, 66

Middle Ages 2, 39, 40, 41, 45, 47, 48, 49, 50, 52, 104, 107, 109, 110, 121, 124, 128

Milan 34, 35

Monica 31, 34

N

Naples 43, 55

Nash 7

Newton 58

nominalism 51, 52, 54

O

Odovacar 38

On Music 38

open-classroom 3

Oswald Arthur Fleming 75

Oxford 2, 45, 46, 47, 60, 71, 72, 73, 74, 103, 119, 127

P

Paideia Proposal 1, 4, 82, 84, 85, 90, 121, 127

Paris 41, 42, 44, 45, 48, 49, 54, 55, 61

Patricius 31

Peirce 8, 64, 65

Pestalozzi 62

Peter the Lombard 45

philosopher-kings 17

Phonics 30

Plato 5, 6, 11, 12, 13, 14, 15, 16, 17, 18, 19, 22, 23, 31, 36, 37, 41, 61

Platonism 36, 55

Pragmatism 1, 8, 9, 57, 63, 64, 65, 66, 68, 121

Progressive 69

progressive 2, 60, 63, 67, 68, 70, 96, 111, 124

Progressivism 8, 9, 57, 67, 68, 93

Ptolemy 42, 48

Pythagoras 13, 31

Q

quadrivium 39, 41, 47, 49, 77, 95, 107, 119, 120, 124

Quintilian 21, 24, 25, 26, 31, 130

R

Ravitch 68, 124

Reading 28, 29, 32, 45, 48, 80, 90, 110, 115

Realism 6, 7, 8, 19, 21, 51, 52, 54, 56

Rhetoric 11, 14, 21, 25, 26, 29, 31, 77, 80, 118, 129

Rhetoric Stage 80

Romulus Augustus 38

Roscellinus 51

Rousseau 58, 60, 61, 62

S

Salerno 43

Sayers 1, 2, 37, 57, 71, 72, 74, 75, 76, 77, 78, 79, 80, 81, 82, 96, 103, 124, 130

Sayers' 1, 2, 37, 71, 75, 81, 82, 124

scholasticism 50, 58, 59

Science 7, 8, 15, 17, 27, 30, 49, 58, 59, 60, 64, 69, 77, 78, 79, 80, 87, 88, 94, 96, 101, 106, 113, 114, 118

Secular Letters 39

shopping mall curriculum 69

Sieve of Classical Philosophy 92

Sizer 81

Social Contract 62

Socrates 6, 10, 11, 12, 13, 14, 18, 22

Socratic 4, 5, 6, 12, 83, 88, 90, 101

Somerville College 73

Sproul 14, 18, 20, 55, 65, 66, 124, 130

St. Augustine 5, 36, 37, 50, 97, 98, 122, 124, 125, 129, 130

Summa theologica 55, 56

Syllogism 48, 106, 115, 116

T

teacher-centered 3, 70, 99

Tertullian 36

Thagaste 31, 33, 35

The Closing of the American Mind 4, 5, 121

The Marriage of Philology and Mercury 39

The Mind of the Maker 75

The Teacher 2, 6, 7, 14, 15, 23, 26, 29, 34, 36, 37, 61, 68, 69, 88, 89, 90, 99, 110, 114, 120, 124

The Troubled Crusade 68, 124

Theology 5, 20, 21, 38, 43, 44, 45, 49, 50, 51, 52, 53, 55, 58, 77, 79, 80, 103, 109, 114, 116, 118, 124

Theophrastus 19

Tolkien 73

Trivium 1, 2, 10, 11, 25, 107, 110, 111, 112, 114, 115, 118, 119, 120, 122

trivium 1, 2, 10, 11, 25, 40, 41, 47, 77, 92, 96, 123, 124

truth 5, 6, 7, 9, 12, 13, 15, 36, 37, 38, 51, 56, 61, 64, 65, 66, 68, 75, 80, 84, 93, 119, 123

U

universitas 41, 46

University 5, 8, 13, 42, 43, 44, 45, 46, 47, 52, 55, 64, 65, 67, 72, 73, 83, 84, 121, 123, 127, 129, 130, 131

university 41, 42, 43, 44, 45, 51, 52, 53, 59, 72, 73, 74, 76, 77, 104, 118, 119, 122, 125

Unmoved Mover 5, 20

Up from Liberalism 81, 127

V

Valerius 36

W

Whose Body? 74

William of Champeaux 44, 51

Wilson 1, 39, 57, 71, 81, 82, 96

978-0-595-38169-2
0-595-38169-3

DATE DUE

7/17/08		
7/19/09		
FEB .0 3 2011		

9 780595 381692